DATE DUE

DEMCO 38-296

Conquering Ring Nerves

A Step-by-Step Program
for All Dog Sports

Conquering Ring Nerves

A Step-by-Step Program
for All Dog Sports

Diane Peters Mayer

HOWELL
BOOK
HOUSE

Copyright © 2004 by Wiley Publishing, Inc.

Howell Book House
Published by Wiley Publishing, Inc., Hoboken, New Jersey
Published simultaneously in Canada

For general information about our other products and services, please contact our
Customer Care Department within the United States at (800) 762-2974, outside the
United States at (317) 572-3993 or fax (317) 572-4002.

Wiley also publishes its books in a variety of electronic formats. Some content that
appears in print may not be available in electronic books. For more information about
Wiley products, visit our web site at www.wiley.com.

Library of Congress Cataloging-in-Publication Data:
Peters Mayer, Diane, date.
  Conquering ring nerves : a step-by-step program for all dog sports /
Diane Peters Mayer.
      p. cm.
Includes bibliographical references and index.
  ISBN 0-7645-4972-3 (cloth: alk. paper)
  1. Dog sports. 2. Dogs—Handling. 3. Performance anxiety. 4.
Self-help techniques. I. Title.
  SF424.P48 2004
  636.7'0811—dc22
                                  2003025515
Manufactured in the United States of America
10 9 8 7 6 5 4 3 2 1

To my husband, Yisrael, and daughters,
Vanessa and Chris, the loves of my life.

For my father, Harry Piotrowsky (1907–2003),
who was waiting to see my first book. I did it, Dad!

And to my beloved Beagle, Benny,
whose rescue started the whole thing.

Contents

Chapter 5

Chapter 6

Chapter 7

Chapter 8

Chapter 9

Competing From Your Core 141

Chapter 10

Stretching: Loosen and Energize 157

Wrap Up 183

APPENDICES

Appendix A

Appendix B

Appendix C

Foreword

As I approach the starting line of an Agility course I'm about to run, I feel a few butterflies, but overall I'm relaxed, confident, and centered. I know I've done my homework and I'm well prepared. My partner, Winston, is sitting calmly at my side, his eyes directed at me, waiting for my signal to begin the run. A few minutes earlier, he had been jumping around, begging for treats and sniffing the ground. When there are only a couple of teams ahead of us, I take some Yoga Breaths and focus on my feet. As a feeling of calm excitement comes over me, Winston settles right in beside me, attentive and ready.

But it hasn't always been that way!

I compete with my Cavalier King Charles Spaniel, Winston, mainly in Agility, but we also compete in Obedience, and soon will be performing in Freestyle. Yet, until Winston and I took Obedience and Agility classes together, I had never performed anywhere doing anything in front of any kind of crowd. Less than a year into our Agility training, there I was going up in front of my peers with a dog, and had to remember which way to go on a course of jumps, tunnels and other obstacles, the sequence of which was planned by someone other than myself. And all this running and remembering and directing had to be done correctly in less than 60 seconds!

We managed to get through the novice and open levels okay, but when we progressed to the excellent level where everything had to be perfect, some real issues began to appear. When I walked up to the start line I was literally shaking, my legs were weak and I was often nauseous. I seemed unable to focus on an entire excellent-level course. I couldn't concentrate, I would forget parts of the course, and I couldn't qualify. My instructors would say things like, "You took your eyes off your dog!" or "Your shoulders were facing that off-course tunnel." Some days I felt weak and had no energy even though I had taken care to maintain proper eating habits and get plenty of rest. I have since learned that this weakness was my body's way of responding to stress. But I loved Agility and had by now developed a passion for something for the first time in my life!

I was determined to become really accomplished at this sport. I sought out the best teachers in the area to sharpen my skills. I added another day,

sometimes two, of classes to my weekly schedule. I began a physical conditioning program for both me and Winston. And I read several books written by
well-known sports psychologists and Olympic champions about training for
and competing in a sport. What I discovered was that they all seemed to agree
that at the highest levels of any sport, there is little difference in physical skill.
The difference is in the mind. Well, I needed to know how to acquire the way
of thinking of a successful competitor. The books talked about relaxing, visualizing, breathing, concentrating and focusing. But none described in detail
how to do it.

One day while searching the Internet for information on how to accomplish these things, I saw a notice about one of Diane's "Competing at Your
Peak" ring nerve seminars. I wrote to Diane and asked to purchase the hand-
outs for the seminar since it was too far away for me to attend. From those
notes, I began teaching myself how to relax, concentrate, visualize and breathe.
Things changed dramatically for me. I began to succeed in finally qualifying on
excellent courses, and over time Winston and I developed into a very consistent team. From the very day I got the premium in the mail I followed the program to the letter, beginning with visualizing the location of the trial and my
upcoming run. I would and still do think about that upcoming run for the six
weeks or two months leading up to it. But the ability to visualize and concentrate did not come easily. It took a lot of practice but I knew I had found the
answer and I was determined. Here at last were instructions on how to achieve
the mind-set that the sports psychologists had been saying serious competitors
need to have.

Diane's regimen taught me how to select and define a program that fit my
particular needs and schedule, so that as I learned how to visualize, concentrate
and fix my energies, I integrated these techniques into my daily training and
my pretrial warm-up. One of the most important aspects of the program for me
is visualization that requires lots of practice, and my training schedule includes
visualizing perfect runs once or twice a day for several days before a weekend
of important trials, including the night before. I practice my breathing every
day in training before I run a course or a sequence of a course so it will be automatic when I'm competing.

Using the program has been the next best thing to having my own personal coach. "Coach" Diane starts the mental training many weeks before the
actual performance with exercises and preparation leading right up to the "big
day." And the program is realistic, taking into account that I might have to do
my stretching exercises while sitting in my car at the trial site or while I'm
walking my dog before his run. The program also included "quickies" for those
occasions when I get to the trial and find things have changed and I'm up first!

The program for conquering ring nerves has enabled me to develop a pretrial routine that puts me and my dog in the "zone." Prior to any run, I spend
about 10 minutes warming up Winston for his run. During that time, I do deep
stretches and Yoga Breathing and I visualize the course several times until it is
clear in my head. I do all of this while I'm walking. Then we relax a little and

go ringside to wait our turn. I learned how to do this from Diane's program. I *never* go into the ring without at least having done several things in preparation: deep stretching accompanied by Yoga Breathing, pressing my thumbs and forefingers together, saying to myself "calm," taking three Yoga Breaths (several times if possible), and focusing on my body, if time allows, or just on my feet. The most interesting part is that Winston is all excited and wild when we get ready to go to the line. Then I take my three Yoga Breaths and watch him settle right down and home in on me with just a little twitch of excitement. It's as though the serenity goes through my body, down the leash into his body. If the first three breaths don't do it, I take three more until I see him calm down.

Since I started using the program, Winston and I have progressed to competing at the highest levels of our sport, Agility. Winston has earned AKC's highest Agility title, Master Agility Champion (MACH) three times and he is the only Cavalier to do so, and one of fewer than 100 dogs in the country to have done so. Winston is AKC's Top Agility Cavalier for 2000 and 2002, and the twentieth dog of all dogs in the country in double qualifications for 2002. He is the top Cavalier in the Front and Finish rankings for 2002. He earned USDAA's Master Agility Dog (MAD) and Master Jumpers (JM) title this year. Last year, he earned USDAA's Master Relay (RM) title. He holds UKC's Agility Champion title, and AKC and WWKC Obedience CDs.

When Diane published the Audio Ring Nerve Program, I was probably the first to buy it. I purchased it right before the AKC National competition in November 2002. At the competition, we had a total of five runs, over three days. Each night before I went to sleep I went through a "Quickie Stress-Buster" exercise, then fell asleep visualizing one of our great runs from a previous trial. At that national competition, we ran all five runs fast and clean and came in 22nd out of 128 dogs in our division. Not bad for a little Cavalier among all those Shelties. And not bad for a handler who three years before was scared out of her wits every time she stepped up to the line.

But more important than these symbols of success is that every run is now a thrill. I no longer feel weak, scared or apprehensive or forget where to go on the course. When we run, I feel almost like I'm floating. I rarely have to think about the course. Many times after a great run I will say to a friend, "Did we do all the obstacles?" And of course, we did!

Winston and I have started in Freestyle and I expect to use the same "zoning" techniques that I use for Agility and Obedience. And I use the same techniques I learned from the program in my everyday life when faced with stressful situations. Thanks "Coach" Diane, for this great program that has helped me conquer my ring nerves. You have given me and countless others the tools to accomplish our goals and turn our dreams into reality.

Marie Logue

Marie lives in Florida and competes in Agility, Obedience and Freestyle with her two Cavalier King Charles Spaniels: MACH 3 Winston, CD, MAD, RM, JM, U-ACHX, and GiGi, CD, MX,MXJ, U-ACH.

Acknowledgments

Bringing a book to completion is truly a collaborative effort. I've been very lucky to have the help, support and love of many people. The following individuals have my deepest gratitude and thanks:

Jacky Sach, my agent, for submitting my idea to Howell, listening to me work through first-time author jitters and taking time out of her day to participate in a photo shoot. Dale Cunningham, executive editor, for her backing and belief in this project. How lucky I am to have Margaret H. Bonham, as my editor. She brings her talents and perspective as a published author as well as a competitive handler to the editing process.

I am so grateful to Marie Logue for writing the foreword. Marie demonstrates that with steely determination and practice, the *Conquering Ring Nerves* program is an effective tool for overcoming performance anxiety. To special friend and gifted dog trainer Pam Dennison, who taught me how to understand and train my Benny and asked me to present the first seminars at her facility, thanks for being supportive, reading some of the text and helping set up the photo shoots. Ali Brown along with Acacia and Montana, and Diane Zdrodowski with Bentley's help, were perfect photographic models. My appreciation to Mike Bailey, decathlete and personal trainer, for his interview and for giving me the idea for "Blue Skies." My dog-walking buddy, Pam Bodenhorn is a true friend who listened to lots of kvetching when the going got tough, had great suggestions for enhancing the book and helped with her computer when mine misbehaved.

Conquering Ring Nerves was also a family affair. Dr. Nathaniel Mayer and Charlene Mayer, BSN, MHA, gave their expertise and offered suggestions to the text. My darling daughters, Vanessa and Chris, took photos, and Vanessa, a personal trainer, also supplied the stretching exercises and information on the *core*. Even more importantly, they cheered me on throughout the process. To my husband, Yisrael, whose ongoing support with research, reading and editing, helped me stay sane and meet my deadline—yes, darling, you can have your life back now!

My deepest appreciation to the handlers who allowed me to use their ring nerve stories to illustrate the text. As much as my program helped the handlers and their beautiful dogs I've worked with over the years, they in turn contributed to my growth as a coach, presenter and author. To them all, I say thank you.

How to Use the Conquering Ring Nerves Program

Conquering Ring Nerves is a self-help program containing practical information, active and written exercises and techniques used by handlers who compete in a variety of dog sports with great success.

To get the maximum results from the program, use the following guidelines:

1. Read through the Table of Contents to get an overall idea of what each chapter contains.

2. Work on the chapters in the order they appear because many of the exercises build on each other. For example, the breathing patterns you'll learn in Chapter 2 will be used in subsequent chapters.

3. Read each chapter before working on the exercises to familiarize yourself with its contents.

4. Read over each exercise and technique two or three times before beginning to practice it.

5. Take your time learning and practicing the exercises in each chapter. Then move on to the next chapter.

6. For great results, make practice part of your daily routine.

7. Work through the entire program, then choose the exercises and techniques you like and find most effective.

8. Keep a Ring Nerves Journal to chart progress, add information, exercises, make comments, and so on. I recommend a three-hole loose-leaf binder that will also allow you to keep photocopies of the written exercises. Be sure to date all materials so you can look back to see how far you've progressed.

9. Open yourself to the program. Some information may be new, and a number of exercises may present initial difficulty. Though it is tough to make changes, enjoy the process of becoming a strong, confident competitor.

10. If you have health concerns, please see your physician before beginning this program.

Introduction

Dear Handler,

The book you hold in your hands contains a coaching program that can free you from the manacles of ring nerves. *Conquering Ring Nerves* will show you how to calm yourself when you're under the pressure of competing, give you techniques to help you remain focused no matter what is going on inside or outside of the ring, boost your self-esteem, mentally rehearse your blue ribbon performance and more. The Ring Nerve Desensitization Program and Training Diary will help you keep yourself on track during training and competitions. Further reading and resource lists are included so you can take your training beyond the scope of this book.

Ring nerves are a mind-body condition and *Conquering Ring Nerves* offers a multidimensional approach, with exercises and techniques adapted from a number of disciplines: psychology, sports psychology, yoga, meditative practices, physical fitness and theater arts. It will take determination, hard work and practice, the very discipline that characterizes the effort you make in turning your dog into a competitor. Now, it's time to begin to train yourself.

I have been developing the program throughout my years as a psychotherapist and life coach, successfully treating people with anxiety, panic attacks and performance anxiety. Business people, athletes, singers, artists, writers and equestrians have benefited from the program. In 1999, I adapted the exercises and techniques to meet the needs of competitive dog handlers. I started Competing At Your Peak, after my dog's trainer asked me to coach her to eliminate her ring nerves and run seminars in her training facility for other competitive handlers. Suddenly, I found myself in a new and wonderful business, helping great handlers and their dogs to find success and have fun in the ring.

But the real beginnings of this program come out of my own anxious experiences. I suffered from performance anxiety for many years. It tripped me up and held me back on tennis courts, while showing horses as a novice rider and in public speaking. So, though I do not compete with my dog, I have first-hand knowledge of what ring nerves feel like and the effects of their fallout. I know how anxiety can thwart success and take the enjoyment out of participating in an activity one loves. I set out to change myself from a nervous wreck into a confident human being who could undertake and enjoy any challenge I set my sights on. I know that performance anxiety can be accepted, faced and conquered. I did it, and with *Conquering Ring Nerves*, you can overcome performance anxiety too.

Throughout the book are real stories from handlers who generously allowed their experiences to be used. Many were Ring Nerve Seminar participants, a few were private clients and others who contributed had used the Ring Nerve audio program or were subscribers to my online newsletter. I thank them from the bottom of my heart. Names have been changed, and many individual stories have been combined to insure confidentiality and better illustrate the text.

Begin your journey now to become the handler of your dreams. Your dog will thank you! And I'll be with you every step of the way.

Happy training,
Diane Peters Mayer

Chapter 1

Anxiety: A Force to Be Reckoned With

No pressure, no diamonds.

Mary Case

IN THIS CHAPTER

- Anxiety
- Fear vs. Anxiety
- The Nervous System
- Parts of the Brain
- The Autonomic Nervous System
- Fight or Flight Response
- Beginning to Face Your Ring Nerves

Jane had been showing for almost a year in competition obedience with her Springer Spaniel, Goldie. Jane signed up for basic obedience classes and Goldie proved to be eager and smart; she loved the training. Jane was hooked after the first few lessons and knew she wanted to become a competitive handler. As the first show approached, Jane was hit with a case of nerves such as she'd never experienced before. She was in a panic, and Goldie, picking up on Jane's anxiety, vomited in the ring during a heeling pattern. And it was downhill from then on. No matter how much she and Goldie trained, each show became one mortifying experience after another. And Goldie, once so keen, now had her own case of canine jitters.

ANXIETY

Anxiety is a normal and important facet of being human. However, anxiety has negative connotations. Many people spend time and money trying to eradicate it. Certainly, it is an ever-present and necessary component in the competitive dog show arena. We need that tension to be able to succeed and reach our personal best. Anxiety must be present to have the spark and vitality in competition, but we need to channel it into a great performance.

When anxiety becomes severe, debilitating and chronic, it breaks down the handler's ability to transfer her training from class to the competition ring. It can limit or block any chance for success. And the pressure is intense! Handlers are "on stage." Handlers are seen, compared, evaluated and scored. They depend on their canine partner to come through in tricky and tough ring situations. From Agility to Obedience to Breed, Flyball, Rally-O and Freestyle, competing can be very intimidating.

FEAR VS. ANXIETY

We often use the words *fear* and *anxiety* interchangeably, but they have two different definitions. Fear is something specific and describable. For example, you get out of your car and turn to see a truck hurtling toward you at 60 miles an hour. The fear of being hit, hurt or killed can be explained in specific terms. You react by trying to jump out of the way. Anxiety, on the other hand, is non-specific and intangible in nature. For example, you get out of your car at a competition site, and when you see the building where the show is, you recall the last time when your handling was miserable, you panicked in the ring and your dog did not qualify. You become anxious, convinced that this scenario will repeat itself, but you can only imagine what might occur. Not being able to prepare for the unexpected makes our feelings of dread very difficult to cope with. Throughout the book, we will be using *fear* and *anxiety* in place of each other, because many handlers do.

RING NERVES

Ring nerves affect handlers in various ways. Many have given up competing, even though they love working with their dogs. Others still show, but are unable to achieve high scores and titles. Some may be getting the scores, but do so without enjoyment. New handlers are often fearful to begin competing.

Let's look at Jane again. Jane is actually a composite of three handlers who had either stopped competing or who were contemplating quitting before they entered the Ring Nerve Program. These handlers now compete in a variety of dog sports. We'll follow Jane from chapter to chapter, charting her progress from nervous wreck to confident competitor.

Pre-show

The following is an example of Jane's preshow anxiety and how it leads to ring nerves. Anticipatory anxiety is often worse than the actual experience because imagination can run amok. For example, the moment Jane thinks about competing, two things occur: She remembers her last appalling performance, and in the same instance begins to worry about what *might* happen in the future, weeks or months before she will even step into the ring.

Entering the Show

Jane decides to enter a show and immediately feels some trepidation. She's experienced anxiety in past trials. Chronically low scores and NQs plagued her in the past. Jane relives humiliating past show experiences in her mind as if they were taking place now.

At the same time, she worries that history will repeat itself, and the "what ifs" begin:

What if Goldie throws up again?
What if I feel like throwing up when I'm in the ring?
What if people I know are there and I mess up?
What if my nerves are ruining my dog?

As these thoughts and worries continue, her nerves build inexorably toward the day of the show. Jane will be a nervous wreck, taking another hit to her already low self-esteem and feeling incapable of ever winning.

Anticipating the Show

This increased anxiety permeates every aspect of Jane's life up to the day of competition and manifests in a variety of symptoms:

- Difficulty sleeping and/or having nightmares
- Loss of appetite or overeating
- Chronic headaches and stomach upsets
- Feeling tired and irritable weeks before a show
- Inability to concentrate
- Training sessions fraught with anxiety

Training Woes

In dog training classes, Jane compares herself to other handlers and their dogs. These crushing negative mental tapes are playing all the time now:

> *I'll never be successful in the ring.*
> *I always fail.*
> *Goldie can't measure up.*

Why am I doing this?

As the show date approaches, Jane questions why she pursues competing, because it's just too painful. Her symptoms have intensified, creating terrible stress for Goldie. Jane thinks she'll have to give up competition, which she is passionate about, because the anxiety is killing her.

The Night Before

The night before the show, Jane's symptoms spike. She has stomach problems and a persistent headache. She can't eat, is irritable and feels tense. She's never been to the show site, and that's making her even more anxious. Jane rechecks the directions and map compulsively. Her stress increases.

Packing for the show is an enormous physical strain. Jane has been binging on junk food over the last week and her clothes feel tight. She can't find anything to wear and thinks she looks fat and ugly.

Jane goes to bed early, but can't fall asleep. She mentally replays the last show with all the embarrassment she felt about her performance, unable to shut these thoughts off. Since she has to rise early for a long drive, Jane worries that she'll be competing on no sleep, so she watches the clock off and on most of the night. Jane manages to doze for a few hours and wakes with a sense of dread.

Going to the Show

Jane's stomach is a mess; she can't eat but drinks her usual two cups of coffee to wake up. In the car, Jane's negative thoughts are running at full speed. She puts on music to relax but it doesn't help. On the way she makes frequent stops at fast-food restaurants to use the bathroom.

The Show

As anxiety mounts to the day of the competition, its physical and mental symptoms become very difficult to control. Jane's ring nerves have intensified to such a degree that she has a feeling of impending doom, knowing another disaster is about to happen.

Entering the Show Site

Jane's stomach knots as she pulls into the parking lot. She tenses her body to push away the fear and grips the steering wheel to gain some control before she exits the car.

As she enters the building, the noise and commotion hit her. Her stomach churns and she feels nauseous, but she gets her number and begins to set up. Jane contemplates scratching and leaving, but that will only make her feel worse, so she grits her teeth and stays.

Pre-Ring Jitters

Jane checks out the rings and judges, but just watching the other competitors only heightens her anxiety. She looks at the running order, sees that it's almost time and begins warming up Goldie. Goldie is inattentive, and Jane's apprehension increases even more, reinforcing what she already believes: they don't have a chance and will NQ as usual. In the on-deck position, Jane finds it difficult to breathe. Her legs tremble and her heart pounds. She feels out of control and at any moment may lose it.

The Ring

When the judge asks if she is ready, Jane's nerves send her into a panic attack. She seizes up and can't concentrate. She has difficulty hearing and understanding the judge's commands. Jane emotionally shuts down to cope with the panic, disconnecting from the event and from Goldie. Jane fulfills her prophecy—they NQ.

The Result

Jane is heartbroken and can't see a way out. Her fears have eroded her self-confidence and belief in her abilities. This is her last show. She stops competing, but continues to check out listings for a "Show and Go" or something equally nonthreatening. But there is no safe event, because even just thinking about going into a ring starts her panic. It's at this point, feeling isolated from the sport she loves and depressed about her situation, that Jane takes the first steps to turn herself around to get back into competition.

Summary of Jane's Experience

Jane's case is typical of severe ring nerves. Readers may see some of their own experiences in her story. Competing is difficult. It takes time, patience and discipline. Unless handlers can cope with performance anxiety, ring nerves will block their road to success.

A Handler's Tale

Ruth attended a Ring Nerve Seminar because severe body tension was causing her and her sighthound difficulties in Obedience. Though the dog was incredible in practice, as soon as he entered the ring he would turn from her and begin to sniff the ground, and Ruth found it almost impossible to get his attention for the rest of their event. Needless to say, Ruth was terribly disappointed in their scores. She asked a friend to watch their performance during the next show. The friend reported that as soon as the judge asked if the handler was ready, the blood drained from Ruth's face and it became very tense and stiff. Her mouth turned down and her eyes bulged.

The friend stated that Ruth's face looked like a death mask. No wonder her poor dog turned away and refused to engage!

Ring nerves also have a powerful impact on your canine partner. The dog observes the handler's physical, mental and emotional state. If a handler is cheerful and excited in training sessions, most dogs think: *Wow! This is great! I love it! Let's keep doing it!* But when show time comes, if instead of that wonderful smile the handler flashed in training class, a grimace covers her face, the dog thinks: *Whoa! What's the matter with her? If things look this bad, I'm out of here!*

WHAT'S HAPPENING TO ME?

Anxiety affects every aspect of our mind and body. To get the most out of this book's exercises and techniques, you need to understand how it works. You'll need to know a little about the nervous system and why you just can't "think" them away. Understanding and accepting performance anxiety is a major step in combating it.

THE NERVOUS SYSTEM

The nervous system is the body's complex organizer. It controls every aspect of living from movement of limbs, organ function and breathing, to thinking, emotions and reactions to our environment. It is divided into the *central nervous system*, which consists of the spinal cord and the brain, and the *peripheral nervous system*, which is found outside of the brain and spinal cord and consists of two major divisions: the *somatic nervous system*, which sends sensory information to the central nervous system, and the *autonomic nervous system*, which automatically performs basic human functions (such as muscle action of the heart) without conscious thought. The autonomic nervous system is influenced by emotions; for example, anxiety about competing can get your heart racing. This system is divided into three parts, two of which, the *sympathetic* and *parasympathetic*, we will examine a little later in this chapter. A closer look at these two systems will give us a greater understanding of how ring nerves function.

The Central Nervous System

The central nervous system is divided into the *brain*, which is located in the brain cavity, and the *spinal cord*, located in the vertebral cavity. It is home to over 100 billion neurons (nerve cells) that carry information throughout the body by receiving and transmitting electrical impulses. Let's look at these two divisions.

The Spinal Cord

The spinal cord, made up of nerve tissue, is protected by the vertebrae of the spinal column. It is the major pathway for information between the brain and peripheral nervous system. Messages in the brain are transmitted by spinal nerves to muscles and joints, which affects movement, and to glands that secrete hormones, including epinephrine and norepinephrine, which may elicit the "fight or flight" response.

The Brain

The extraordinarily complex human brain weighs approximately two pounds and has the enormous task of communicating to and controlling every organ and bodily operation. It communicates and controls the human body through hormones and electrical impulses that run down the spinal column.

This human supercomputer consists of:

- *The brain stem (reptilian brain)*, where our "fight or flight" survival response is found, controls automatic functions such as breathing, heart rate, blood pressure and functioning of internal organs for digestion, urination, etc.

- *The cerebellum* has two hemispheres. It is located behind the brain stem and controls and regulates movement, posture and balance.

- *The cerebrum*, the largest part of the brain, controls our higher functions, including thought, logic, language, voluntary movement and perception. It is divided into two hemispheres: the creative right side and the logical left side. The cerebrum also contains the *limbic system*, whose main function is the control of emotions with another of its sections, the *hippocampus*, governing memory.

The Peripheral Nervous System

The peripheral nervous system, linked to the central nervous system by cranial and spinal nerves, has two branches.

- The somatic nervous system carries sensory information to the brain and spinal cord via neurons that are contained in blood and lymph vessels, internal organs and sense organs, as well as muscles, tendons and the skin. The information these neurons carry communicate to the brain what is going on internally, as well as what's happening in the external surroundings, so it can prepare an appropriate response.

- The autonomic nervous system operates unconsciously and controls and regulates involuntary body systems and organs, such as heart rate, blood pressure and respiration, by sending out hormones and electrical impulses. If you walk into a show site where you previously experienced an anxiety attack and begin to have the same feelings as before, the sensory information will signal a threat and then the autonomic nervous system will trigger its defense, the fight or flight response. This system is divided into two complimentary branches.

The Autonomic Nervous System

The autonomic nervous system regulates body systems and organs by sending out hormones and electrical impulses. For example, it can rev up or slow down breathing depending on the body's need. This system is divided into two branches:

- The sympathetic nervous system is responsible for readying the body to meet dangerous or threatening situations, which is known as the fight or flight response.

- The parasympathetic nervous system is activated when the danger is over and returns the body to its normal resting condition to wait for the next threat.

THE FIGHT OR FLIGHT RESPONSE

Now that you've read about how the nervous system functions, you can see that all its parts are interrelated, so when ring nerves strike, its effects are felt both mentally and physically. What follows is an explanation of the body's reaction during the fight or flight response, and then we'll see what happens when fight or flight is activated at a competition.

When a real or perceived threat occurs the brain immediately sends messages to the sympathetic nervous system, triggering major bodily changes to prepare for fight or flight:

- Heart rate and blood pressure increase to pump more blood into the brain, muscles and organs to meet the threat.
- Blood flow decreases to extremities, the hands and feet, which are not as important for survival.
- Breathing becomes rapid to obtain more oxygen.
- Muscles tense, preparing for action.
- Adrenaline and other stress hormones are released into the bloodstream.
- The liver sends stored sugar into the bloodstream to meet increased need for energy.
- Pupils dilate to let in more light to heighten awareness of surroundings.
- The body sweats to cool itself for the heat of battle or escape.
- Saliva production is reduced to suspend digestion, and "dry mouth" occurs.
- Emptying of bowel and bladder takes place to clean the body for action.

FIGHT OR FLIGHT AT A COMPETITION

Let's look at what happens when you're at a show and ring nerves strike:

- You interpret stepping into the competition ring as perilous.
- Your brain gets this message and charges up all systems to meet the danger.
- Your heart starts pounding rapidly.
- Hands and feet may feel cold and clammy.
- Rapid, shallow chest breathing begins, which may lead to hyperventilation.
- Your entire body is extremely tense and stiff, making you feel awkward and off balance.
- You're slammed with an adrenaline rush when stress chemicals are released into the bloodstream.
- You become hyperaware of surroundings and noise.
- A "cold sweat" may occur.
- You may get "cottonmouth."
- While waiting around you make frequent trips to the bathroom.

Uh-oh, I feel panicky.

Are we going to NQ again?

Now, you're not going to pay attention?!

If you don't scratch and still decide to enter the show in spite of anxiety, your mind and body will be affected: your logic, reasoning, memory and perception will not function properly. So it's no wonder that you can't remember the course, hear or understand the calls, connect with your dog or even recall what happened when you're done.

Finally, the danger is over and you're on the way home, and the parasympathetic nervous system is activated to return the body to its normal, nonaroused, resting condition. But if you experience ring nerves as a constant threat because of another impending competition, then your body will never fully return to a relaxed state. Stress levels will drop to some degree after a competition, but if thinking about this show, past shows or future shows trigger anxiety, then the whole cycle repeats itself without leaving home. This is ring nerves in its chronic form.

WHY ME?

Most people who suffer from anxiety in some form question why it's happening to them. These handlers often vent their frustrations in ring nerve seminars and e-mail messages. They believe that no one else in their training class suffers the way they do or is so blocked and they want to desperately understand. "Why me?" they lament.

To them, ring nerves are illogical and inexplicable, as are their feelings of dread and doom about entering a dog show. They know that going into the ring is not dangerous. If they NQ, nothing is really going to happen to them. No one is perfect in the ring! Though the symptoms seem absurd, the anguish and pain is real. There is no one theory on severe anxiety and its causes. There's no one definitive reason for anxiety to surface. Anxiety operates on many levels. The following are only a few of the possible reasons:

- Hereditarily predisposed to anxiety disorders
- Learned anxiety from parents
- Childhood factors: critical/rigid/overprotective/neglectful parents
- Traumatic experiences
- Medical conditions

Later, in the Chapter 6, *The Confidence Game*, we'll expand on the causes of anxiety.

RING NERVE CHECKLIST

The following exercise is helpful to begin the process of combating ring nerves. It helps you take a long, hard look at what happens to you and your dog during competition.

1. Read the following list and check off all that apply to you.
2. When you're finished, read what you've written and try to evoke a feeling of anxiety.
3. Rate your symptoms on the Ring Nerve Anxiety Scale below.
4. We'll be using this information in a later chapter, so keep it at hand.
5. Relax for a few minutes.

Ring Nerve Symptoms

Do you experience any of the following prior to competition, during competition, or in between shows? Check off all that apply and include any other symptoms.

Physical Symptoms

__Rapid heartbeat

__Dry mouth

__Shaky limbs

__Tension in the head, neck and shoulders

__Headache

__Tight facial muscles

__Nausea, diarrhea, vomiting

__Tightening in the throat

__Shallow breathing, hyperventilation

__Trembling

Mental and Emotional Symptoms

__Loss of concentration

__Feeling faint

__Feeling overwhelmed

__Feeling out of control

__Feeling tearful

__Feeling helpless

__Feeling anger

__Feeling shame

__Feeling terrified of the ring

__Panic attacks

Other: _____

_____

_____

_____

_____

Competition Problems

Do any of the following take place during training or while you're in the ring?
Check off all that apply and include other experiences.

__Disconnect from your dog

__Fear that your dog will make a mistake and NQ

__Getting angry at your dog for a poor showing

__Fear of being negatively evaluated

__ Training well, but showing badly

__Obsessing about past performances

__Experiencing anxiety during training sessions

__Negatively comparing yourself to other handlers

__Fearing the judge

__Stop showing

Other: _____

_____

_____

_____

RING NERVE ANXIETY SCALE

10_____Panic city!!!

9_____How do I get off this runaway train?!

8_____No place to run, no place to hide

7_____They're he-e-ere!

6_____Not feeling so hot

5_____Feel the build

4_____Uh-Oh!

3_____First twinges

2_____So far so good

1_____Feelin' cool

0_____No ring nerves in sight

Does your dog do any of the following during training or competition?

__Avoid looking at you during competition

__Shut down in training sessions

__Shut down in the ring

__Lag or respond to signals too slowly

__Get frantic and out of control

__React to your ring nerves

__NQ often

__Not want to compete

Other: _____

_____

_____

_____

_____

SAMPLE CHECKLIST

Following is an example of one handler's checklist.

Ring Nerve Symptoms

Do you experience any of the following prior to competition, during competition, or in between shows? Check off all that apply and include any other symptoms.

Physical Symptoms

_X_ Rapid heartbeat

__Dry mouth

_X_ Shaky limbs

_X_ Tension in the head, neck and shoulders

__Headache

_X_ Tight facial muscles

__Nausea, diarrhea, vomiting

_X_ Tightening in the throat

_X_ Shallow breathing; Hyperventilation

_X_ Trembling

Mental and Emotional Symptoms

_X_ Loss of concentration

_X_ Feeling faint

_X_ Feeling overwhelmed

_X_ Feeling out of control

__Feeling tearful

__Feeling helpless

__Feeling anger

_X_ Feeling terrified of the ring

_X_ Panic attacks

Other: *Panic hits the night before a show. Changed training schools and have no support group now to go to shows with, which adds to anxiety. I'd rate all of the above on the Ring Nerve Anxiety Scale as 7 to 10.*

Competition Problems

Do any of the following take place during training or while you're in the ring? Check off all that apply and include other experiences.

_X_ Disconnect from your dog

_X_ Fear that your dog will make a mistake and NQ

__Getting angry at your dog for a poor showing

_X_ Fear of being negatively evaluated

_X_ Training well, but showing badly

_X_ Obsessing about past performances

__Experiencing anxiety during training sessions

_X_ Negatively comparing yourself to other handlers

_X_ Fearing the judge

__Stop showing

Other: *Everything in this list is between 6 to 9.*

Does your dog do any of the following during training or competition?

X Avoid looking at you during competition

__ Shut down in training sessions

X Shut down in the ring

X Lag or respond to signals too slowly

__ Get frantic and out of control

X React to your ring nerves

X NQ often

__ Not want to compete

Other: *None of these are during training, all during competing, although not in Agility, probably because I don't do Agility as seriously as Competition Obedience. During Obedience my anxiety level is between 8 and 10.*

Ring nerves in its chronic state can lead to exhaustion, a host of mental and emotional symptoms, such as depression, feelings of worthlessness and helplessness and even physical ailments like hypertension. If these occur, giving up competing may seem like the only way out. It's not!

THE PROCESS OF CONQUERING RING NERVES

Your way to overcome ring nerves will require determination, discipline and practice. It won't be easy, because changing anxiety-ridden responses is difficult to do. The road to competing at your peak will be filled with many obstacles and setbacks. You may take two steps forward and one step back. But remember, you'll be moving ahead and getting closer to being a successful handler.

It *is* possible to stop ring nerves, connect with your dog, keep the necessary tension that competition requires, learn to concentrate and be emotionally open to your event. Your journey to freedom from the anxiety that blocks success begins with this book.

FURTHER READING

Martin M. Anthony, et al. *The Shyness and Social Anxiety Workbook: Proven Techniques for Overcoming Your Fears.* New Harbinger Publishing, 2000.

David Barlow. *Anxiety and Its Disorders: The Nature and Treatment of Anxiety and Panic* (2nd edition). Guilford Press; 2001.

Lucinda Bassett. *From Panic to Power: Proven Techniques to Calm Your Anxieties, Conquer Your Fears, and Put You in Control of Your Life.* Quill, 2001.

Edmund J. Bourne. *The Anxiety & Phobia Workbook* (3rd edition). New Harbinger Publishing, 2000.

Jonathan R. T. Davidson. *The Anxiety Book: Developing Strength in the Face of Fear* Henry Dreher, Riverhead Books, 2003.

Signe A. Dayhoff. *Diagonally-Parked in a Parallel Universe:Working Through Social Anxiety Effectiveness.* Plus Publications, 2000.

Janet I. Decker. *Hypnosis for Stress Reduction* (audio CD). Hypnotherapy Services, 2001.

RESOURCE LIST

National Institute of Mental Health (NIMH) Anxiety Disorders, http://www.nimh. nih.gov/anxiety

Anxiety Disorders Association of America, http://www.adaa.org

The Anxiety Panic Internet Resource, http://www.algy.com/anxiety/anxiety.html

Mental Health: A Report of the Surgeon General; Chapter 4, Anxiety Disorders, http://www.surgeongeneral.gov/library/mentalhealth/chapter4/sec2.html

Dealing with Depression or Anxiety Disorders, http//:www.mentalhealth.com/fr20.htm

Panic Disorder, Panic Attacks and General Anxiety—What You Should Do, http://www.geocities.com/spiroll2

Anxieties.Com: A free Internet self-help site, http://www.anxieties.com

Anxiety and Depression Resource Organization since 1984, http://www.freedomfromfear.com

Chapter 2

The Breath Is the Key

The breath is a bridge between body and mind.

Swami Rama

IN THIS CHAPTER

- Defining Diaphragmatic Breathing (Yoga Breath)
- Why Changing Your Breathing Habits Works
- Breathing Away Ring Nerves
- Practical Uses for Yoga Breath in Training and Competition
- Facing Ring Nerve Symptoms with Yoga Breath

Jane became very conscious of her breath once she understood the connection between breathing and ring nerves. The first thing we worked on was having her begin her day by doing Yoga Breath for a few minutes right before she got up. This is how I wanted her to start if she were going to a show, to take command of the breath even before she got out of bed.

"I absolutely fell in love with Yoga Breath. I teach, and taking control of my breathing helped me in some tough situations in the classroom," Jane says. "It was quite a bit of work getting the breathing down just right, and then becoming conscious of making the switch to Yoga Breath as often as possible. But little by little I began to see a difference in how I felt, especially in dog training class. I had control over my emotions for the first time in ages. I could reduce my tension and nerves anywhere I was.

"Since I stopped competing, class had become hard emotionally because I had to listen to other handlers who regularly entered shows talk about how they had done. That left me feeling that Goldie and I were going nowhere fast. I felt my confidence returning after about three weeks of doing Yoga Breath, and decided to

enter an easy match to practice what I was learning. That alone was a huge victory, but I was determined to do it.

"I used Yoga Breath the night before the match, right before I went to sleep, and it helped me to get more rest than I usually would have. I practiced it in the house before I left, and as soon as I got to the show site. I didn't leave my car until the breathing calmed me. Diane had me breathe again right before I touched Goldie and took her out of the car, and I breathed my way right through the match. I was nervous and we NQ'd, but I was able to keep reducing the tension and never had my anxiety spike like it used to. For the first time in a long time, I felt like we were winners."

BREATHING

We never think about how we breathe, unless something happens like a bad cold. We don't notice that we are breathing shallowly from our chest and often not taking in enough oxygen. Sometimes we even hold our breath without noticing. But when we're in an anxiety-producing situation such as a dog show, we feel the repercussions of our inadequate breathing habits.

The involuntary autonomic nervous system that activates the fight or flight response also controls our lungs and breathing patterns. When we get scared and anxious, our breathing becomes shallow and rapid and we gasp for air, which only heightens the anxiety and increases ring nerve symptoms.

Kenny's Nerves

Kenny competes with his Border Collie, Scout. As a novice, he initially felt some butterflies, but he did not experience ring nerves. He and Scout did quite well. However, as they began to move from novice to higher levels of competition, the stakes changed, and so did Kenny's nerves. His preshow anxiety became so intense that when he was waiting for his turn he felt terrible. Kenny felt so shaky that he couldn't stand still. On the start line, his heart pounded and he began to fear he would have a heart attack. Scout picked up on the ring nerves and became wild when Kenny's anxiety spiked. It was almost impossible to get Scout's full attention or settle her down.

Things started to turn worse and they NQ'd often. Agility, which had seemed like such fun and held the promise of garnering titles, had become a source of frustration and disappointment.

But breathing is also voluntary as well as involuntary. If we wish, we can consciously decide to take a deep breath. It allows us to take direct control of our breathing and override or ease the sympathetic nervous system's fight or flight response. However, you can do this only with training and practice.

Consider Kenny, the agility competitor. As he and his Border Collie, Scout, started improving in agility, his nervousness started. Scout picked up on it and went wild in the ring. Can Kenny do anything?

Yes. The answer lies in *diaphragmatic breathing*, also called *Yoga Breath*: a controlled pattern of breath work based on yoga principles. Yoga Breath uses the diaphragm, not the chest, and will slow Kenny's breathing. Slowing his breathing will slow his mind and body, and change him from a bundle of nerves into a calm and confident competitor.

As soon as Kenny realized breathing had an enormous effect on him and Scout, he made diaphragmatic breathing part of his life. "It's made such a difference," says Kenny. "We're back on track to becoming a great competitive team. Scout settles down quickly and is with me right from the start."

WHAT IS DIAPHRAGMATIC BREATHING (YOGA BREATH)?

The diaphragm is a dome-shaped muscle that separates the chest and abdomen and lies between the heart and lungs. It is connected to the stomach, kidneys, liver, spleen, pancreas, bladder and the small and large intestines. It wraps around the lower ribs and lower vertebrae. When we inhale the diaphragm moves downward and when we exhale it moves upward. This up and down movement impacts upon all the organs in the body with a beneficial effect to promote better blood and lymph flow. The lymphatic system, part of the body's defense mechanism, plays an important role in our immune system, enabling the body to fight infection and disease.

The stressfulness of our lives is evident in our rapid, shallow breathing. It is certainly evident at a dog show. However, when we're able to slow down and deepen and lengthen the breath, our lungs are able to expand to take in more oxygen and release more carbon dioxide. The parasympathetic nervous system turns on to help keep us feeling relaxed and centered. We then transmit our feelings to our dogs.

Breathing Exercise

1. How are you breathing at this moment? Is your breath shallow? Are you taking in enough air? Are you holding your breath?

2. Breathing only through your nose, inhale and exhale slowly and deeply 10 times. How did that feel? Did your body relax?

Lessening Fear

Laurie participated in a ring nerve seminar. "I desperately needed something to help relieve the anxiety that kept me from the focus and concentration necessary to get the most out of any activity that required performance," she says. She was terribly insecure and constantly played mental tapes of her ineptness. "I was consumed with thoughts of making mistakes."

After a rather humiliating experience at an Agility trial, she registered for the seminar. "I knew I had to do something when a 12-year-old competitor had no problem remembering to do the third and final red jump required in a Snooker class, and I forgot to do it because of my nerves!" Laurie said. "I've also got to stop communicating my anxiety to my dog and stressing her out."

Laurie was surprised that she felt an almost immediate lessening of her fear after practicing Yoga Breath for just a few hours at the seminar. "I learned how to cope with anxiety and loss of concentration by just breathing!"

"I still get nervous and make mistakes, but I haven't shut down since I started Yoga Breath," Laurie says. "I'm involved in new activities in environments that have the potential to be very stressful for me and my dog. I'm getting better and I believe my dog is getting better as well. For this, I'm very grateful."

The breathing exercises in this chapter are easy to learn, very effective and offer many benefits, including:

- Activating the parasympathetic nervous system
- Stopping or interrupting the fight or flight response
- Stopping handlers from holding their breath in the ring
- Keeping handlers relaxed in all show circumstances
- Increasing energy
- Heightening concentration and focus
- Allowing all training and knowledge to flow unblocked into performance
- Maintaining a general feeling of well-being

The Power of the Breath

In the book *Science of Breath* (Rama, Ballentine and Hymes, Himalayan Press, 1998), Swami Rama demonstrates the powerful effect on the mind and body of certain breathing techniques. Swami Rama is a yogi raised in the Himalayas who "walked into an American research laboratory" and "Under the most rigorous experimental conditions, simulated death by virtually stopping his brain waves and heart beat . . . yet remained fully conscious of events occurring around him in the laboratory." This amazing feat demonstrates the force of the breath on physical and mental functions.

Think how shallow chest breathing can begin or intensify ring nerves and realize that you can start to conquer performance anxiety just by changing your breathing patterns. Your breathing influences your dog's attitude. You'll find that your dog is a more willing partner when you use diaphragmatic breathing.

Why Breathing Works—An Alternate Explanation

Tarthang Tulku writes in *Tibetan Relaxation: Kum Nye Massage and Movement* (Duncan Baird Publishers, 2003), "Because breathing charts the life rhythms, the way we breathe signals the disposition of our energies. When we are agitated or excited, our breath tends to be uneven and rapid; when we are calm and balanced, our breathing is even, slow and soft. This close relationship between . . . breathing patterns and our energies means that we can alter our mental and physical states by the way we breathe . . . we can calm and balance ourselves simply by breathing slowly and evenly."

One of the remarkable and wondrous aspects of breathing is your ability to take conscious command of it. And when you do, your life will change.

GETTING STARTED USING YOGA BREATH

Learning to control and direct the breath enables you to take charge of physical, mental and emotional functioning while in the most demanding situations. Yoga Breath can be tough to integrate into daily life, but with determination and practice you can do it.

Now it's your turn to learn this extraordinary technique.

1. Find a quiet spot.

2. Have a mat or towel handy.

Training Tip

To make sure you are breathing properly, place one hand on your chest, which should have very little movement. Put the other hand on your abdomen, and feel it pull in and push out as you exhale and inhale.

3. Breathe through your nose only to cleanse and help regulate the breath.

4. Begin with an exhale.

5. Breathe through your diaphragm, not your chest.

6. As you exhale to at least a count of three, the abdomen should gently contract.

7. As you inhale to at least a count of three, the abdomen will expand.

8. Keep your chest as still as possible.

9. Breathing should be slow, smooth and quiet.

10. Concentrate on each breath as it goes in and out of your body.

11. When thoughts come, let them stay for a moment, then gently refocus on the breath.

12. If you lose the rhythm or feel like you're not getting enough air, stop and take a few regular breaths, then continue.

13. Yoga Breath may be uncomfortable at first, but with practice, it will become second nature.

YOGA BREATH PRACTICE EXERCISES

In this series of exercises, you will learn to do Yoga Breath in five positions: prone, sitting with eyes closed, sitting with eyes open, standing and walking. As you begin to use these breathing techniques during training class and at competitions, you will find your anxiety lessening, your ability to focus increasing, and your confidence boosted.

Yoga Breath Prone Position

1. Set the timer for one to two minutes.

2. Lie on your back, on a mat or towel, legs relaxed and slightly apart.

3. If your neck feels uncomfortable, place a small pillow or rolled towel under your head.

Training Tip

Set your clock or use an egg timer and begin with one to two minutes of practice. Slowly increase time to at least five minutes per practice session.

Yoga Breath prone.

4. Rest your arms at your sides, or place one hand on your chest and the other on your abdomen.

5. Close your eyes.

6. Exhale slowly to at least a count of three. Your abdomen should relax and pull in.

7. Inhale slowly to at least a count of three, and feel your abdomen fill.

8. Eventually work up to three to five minutes of practice each session.

9. When you finish, relax for a moment.

10. Practice daily.

Yoga Breath Sitting Eyes Closed

1. Set the timer for one to two minutes.

2. Sit in a chair with both feet flat on the floor, hands resting in your lap.

3. Sit tall and relax your head, neck and shoulders.

4. Close your eyes.

5. Exhale slowly to at least a count of three.

Training Tip

Yoga Breath in the prone position is useful in bed the night before a show to sleep well and wake refreshed. Practice the morning of the show before you get out of bed.

The breath is the key.

6. Inhale slowly to at least a count of three.

7. Keep your chest as still as possible.

8. When you've finished, relax.

9. Work up to three to five minutes of practice.

10. Practice daily.

Yoga Breath Sitting Eyes Open

This exercise has an added element that increases focus.

1. Set the timer for one to three minutes.

2. Sit in a chair with both feet flat on the floor, hands resting in your lap.

Training Tip

When to use Yoga Breath Sitting Eyes Closed:

- In your vehicle at a show
- In restroom at a show
- Sitting around at a show waiting to be called

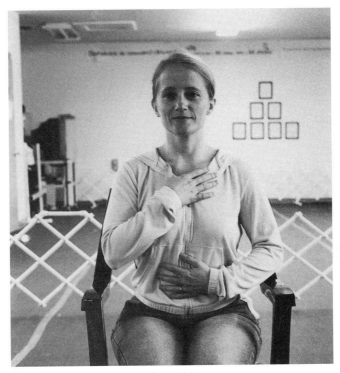

Breathe and focus.

3. Sit tall and relax your head, neck and shoulders.

4. Find something in front of you to focus on: a picture on the wall, a piece of furniture, a photo of your dog, anything at all. Continue to concentrate on your object.

5. If stray thoughts intrude, don't fight them, but gently refocus on your breath.

Training Tip

Practice Yoga Breath Sitting Eyes Open as often as possible at home, work and in training sessions:

- In the house before you leave for a show
- In your vehicle at the show site
- While you're waiting for your number to be called

Training Tip

If you're finding Yoga Breath tough to master, don't force it. Relax into it and keep practicing. Eventually, it will become natural.

6. Exhale slowly to at least a count of three, while looking at your object.

7. Inhale slowly to at least a count of three.

8. Keep your chest as still as possible.

9. Continue to look at your object.

10. Work up to three to five minutes of practice.

11. After you finish, relax and take a moment to consider how you feel.

12. Practice daily.

Was it hard to focus on a point and breathe? If so, don't worry—you'll get it!

Yoga Breath Standing

1. Set the timer for one to three minutes.

2. Stand straight and distribute your weight on both legs to feel balanced.

3. Relax head, neck and shoulders.

4. Focus on something in front of you.

5. Exhale slowly to at least a count of three.

6. Inhale slowly to at least a count of three.

7. Keep focusing on your object.

Training Tip for Sitting, Standing, Walking

Set your clock or use an egg timer and begin with five minutes of practice. Slowly increase time to 10 to 15 minutes per session. Be sure to vary the length of time, for example: one minute sitting, three minutes standing, five minutes walking or seven minutes sitting, two minutes standing, one minute walking, etc.

Yoga breathing while in the on-deck position.

8. Increase practice time to at least five minutes.

9. After you finish, relax.

10. Practice daily.

Was it hard to stand and do Yoga Breath at the same time? If it was, with time it will all come together.

Yoga Breath Walking

1. Set the timer for three to five minutes.

2. Stand straight and distribute your weight on both legs to feel balanced.

3. Relax head, neck and shoulders.

4. As you begin Yoga Breath, start walking slowly.

5. Focus your attention on each breath as you walk.

6. If you get distracted, gently return to your breath.

7. Increase practice time to ten minutes per session.

8. When time is up, sit down, relax and see how you feel.

9. Practice daily.

Was practicing Yoga Breath in various positions difficult? Did it come easier as you went along? With practice, Yoga Breath will begin to work its magic.

Training Tip

Practice Yoga Breath Sitting to Standing until you experience no break in concentration.

ADVANCED YOGA BREATH—PUTTING IT ALL TOGETHER

Now we're going to combine *sitting, standing* and *walking* so you can make a smooth transition from one to the other. The object is to make a quick mental shift without breaking concentration.

Yoga Breath Sitting to Standing

1. Set desired time.
2. Sit comfortably in a chair, feet flat on the floor.
3. Relax head, neck and shoulders.
4. Keep your eyes open.
5. Begin Yoga Breath.
6. Put all of your attention on the breath going in and out of your body.
7. Focus on a point in the room.
8. If you get distracted, gently come back to the breath.
9. Keep breathing slowly and smoothly.
10. Now, stand while keeping Yoga Breath going.
11. Distribute your weight on both legs to feel balanced.
12. Make sure your neck, head and shoulders are relaxed.
13. Continue Yoga Breath.
14. If you get distracted, gently refocus on your breath.
15. When you're finished, sit down, relax and see how you feel.
16. Practice daily.

Were you able to keep your focus? Try not to force it, but relax into the exercise.

Training Tip

- When you become comfortable with the exercises, begin to include your dog in practice sessions. This is important preparation for the show ring.
- Practice in various locations: home, work, training class, at play.

Yoga Breath Sitting to Standing to Walking

1. Set desired time.

2. Sit comfortably in a chair, feet flat on the floor.

3. Relax head, neck and shoulders.

4. Keep your eyes open.

5. Begin Yoga Breath.

6. Stand and continue Yoga Breath for about 10 seconds.

7. Now, begin to walk, focusing on each breath.

8. Continue walking and breathing.

9. If you get distracted, gently refocus on your breath as it goes in and out of your body.

10. When time is up, relax and take a few minutes to see how you feel.

11. Practice daily.

Training Tip

Take command of your event at the start by using Yoga Breath, even though your anxiety is spiking and the judge is calling you into the ring. Here's how: practice relaxing mind and body almost instantly by *exhaling* slowly through your nose, a process that will take three seconds; then on the *inhale*, enter the ring. Remember, this will take practice, practice, practice!

Training Tip

If you compete in Competition Obedience or Conformation, you will be able to do Yoga Breath for much of your event. In Agility, or other sports where you're moving quickly, you may have to revert to chest breathing, but the calming effects of Yoga Breath will stay with you.

Alternate Nostril Breathing

Of the major pathways that receive oxygen into the body, the nose is an extremely important organ whose many purposes include regulating, filtering and warming the air, directing airflow and recording the sense of smell. Breathing through the nose stimulates the brain, which affects the nervous system and psychological functioning.

In *Alternate Nostril Breathing*, an exercise based on yoga, you'll be closing off one nostril and breathing through the other. As you do this, you'll find yourself getting calmer, yet feeling energized with a sense of well-being.

Where and When to Practice Yoga Breath

- Watching TV
- At the computer
- In your vehicle
- At your desk
- Doing the dishes
- While playing other sports
- At the movies
- Walking in the house
- Walking your dog
- Walking at work
- At sporting events
- Before you go to sleep
- Every time you train your dog
- At every competition

A Handler's Tale

Sam competed in Agility, Obedience and Breed, and suffered from severe preshow anxiety. "Weeks before the competition, my anxiety would build until show time, because I'm very competitive and a perfectionist, so I was always worried about making mistakes and looking bad.

"I was so irritable waiting for the show date that I was impossible to live with, verbally jumping at family and snapping at people at work. I've always had a short fuse and competing only makes it worse. If we didn't do well I got angry at my dog even though I knew it wasn't his fault. I would tell myself to cool it: it's only a dog show. But that didn't work. I began the Ring Nerve Program and learned Yoga Breath. It was a wake-up call for me and Alternate Nostril Breathing really changed my life. I finally have control over my nerves and temper, in all areas of my life. When I learned to calm myself, our scores got much better and I actually began to enjoy myself. My dog is relieved too."

1. Sit in a chair, feet flat on the floor.

2. Exhale through your nose and pull in your stomach.

3. Place your right thumb against your right nostril. Hold the right nostril closed with your thumb while inhaling through the left nostril, to the count of three.

4. Make the inhale and exhale slow, rhythmic and quiet.

5. Close both nostrils with the thumb and fourth finger on your right hand, and hold for a count of three.

6. Release the right nostril and exhale to a count of three.

7. Inhale through the right nostril, to a count of three.

8. Close both nostrils with the thumb and fourth finger of the right hand and hold for a count of three.

9. Release the left nostril and exhale to a count of three.

10. Inhale with the left nostril to a count of three.

Training Tip

Give yourself time to learn Alternate Nostril Breathing, remembering to keep your breath slow, smooth, and quiet.

Training Tip

- Become aware of how often you hold your breath or breathe shallowly.
- Make a conscious effort to switch to Yoga Breath throughout the day.

11. Close both nostrils and count to three.

12. Open the right nostril and begin again.

13. When you have inhaled and exhaled three times in each nostril (one repetition) take a breath through both nostrils.

14. Repeat the entire exercise for six repetitions, and relax.

15. Practice daily

JANE'S PROGRESS

Jane got back into competition. She entered shows that were as nonthreatening as possible, with no other goal in mind than to practice taking control of her ring nerves through conscious breathing.

"It was a struggle to go into a competition with one goal, *breathing,* and ignore trying to get a perfect performance out of Goldie," Jane says. "But I felt that concentrating only on Yoga Breath was the way we could become good competitors someday. I added Alternate Nostril Breathing to my ring nerve program, and do it in my car right before I enter the building. Sometimes while we're waiting to be called, I do the nostril breathing in the bathroom. It helps me handle my anxiety until it's our turn."

YOGA BREATH AND YOUR RING NERVE SYMPTOMS

In the following exercise, you'll use Yoga Breath's calming quality to help you confront the negative symptoms of ring nerves in order to render them powerless.

1. Set the timer for at least 5 minutes.

2. Take out your Ring Nerve Symptom Checklist (see Chapter 1).

3. Sit in a chair with feet flat on the floor.

4. Relax your head, neck and shoulders.

5. Read over your checklist trying to bring up the feelings your symptoms evoke.

6. Begin Yoga Breath.

7. If you feel any anxiety, don't tense, but breathe into your feelings.

8. Keep reading what you wrote while you're in a relaxed state.

9. Sit back and see how you feel.

10. Now, rate each symptom on the Ring Nerve Anxiety Scale, to see if your levels of anxiety have dropped.

11. Repeat at least twice a week.

Do you feel any difference from the time you first wrote your list? This is an important exercise, because facing your distressing feelings at home in a relaxed state will prepare you to deal with ring nerves when you're in the highly pressured dog show environment.

Practice Yoga Breath daily and it will become second nature, allowing you to turn off anxiety in seconds. Yoga breathing is an important component of many of the exercises and techniques in subsequent chapters. For more information on yoga and breathing, see the recommended reading and resource list below.

Begin practicing and using Yoga Breath today to become the master of your life, both inside and outside of the competitive dog show ring.

RING NERVE ANXIETY SCALE

10	Panic city!!!
9	How do I get off this runaway train?!
8	No place to run, no place to hide
7	They're he-e-ere!
6	Not feeling so hot
5	Feel the build
4	Uh-oh!
3	First twinges
2	So far so good
1	Feelin' pretty cool
0	No ring nerves in sight

FURTHER READING

Alice Christensen. *The American Yoga Association's Beginners Manual*. Fireside, 2002.

Sophie Gabriel. *Breathe for Life: How to Reduce Stress and Enhance Your Fitness*. Basic Health Publications, 2002.

Dharma Singh Khalsa, M.D., and Cameron Stauth. *Meditation as Medicine*. Pocket Books, 2001.

Gurucharan Singh Khalsa and Yogi Bhajan. *Breathwalk: Breathing Your Way to a Revitalized Body, Mind, and Spirit*. Broadway Books, 2000.

John C. Meneghini. *The Healing Art of Conscious Breathing* (unabridged audio CD). Sadhana Concepts, 2002.

Fred L. Miller. *How to Calm Down: Three Deep Breaths to Peace of Mind*. Warner Books, 2003.

A. G. Mohan. *Yoga for Body, Breath and Mind: A Guide to Personal Reintegration*. Random House, 2002.

Swami Rama. *Path of Fire and Light: Advanced Practices of Yoga*. Himalayan Institute Press, 1999.

Swami Rama, Alan Hymes, et al. *Science of Breath: A Practical Guide*. Himalayan Institute Press, 1998.

Richard Rosen. *The Yoga of Breath: A Step by Step Guide to Pranayama*. Shambhala Publications, 2002.

Sivanda Yoga Center, Vishnu Devananda. *The Sivananda Companion to Yoga: A Complete Guide to the Physical Postures, Breathing Exercises, Diet, Relaxation, and Meditation Techniques of Yoga*. Fireside, 2000.

Tarthang Tulku. *Tibetan Relaxation Kum Nye Massage and Movement*. Duncan Baird Publishers, 2003.

RESOURCE LIST

Breath Work Information, http://www.naturalhealthweb.com/topics/subtopics/breath_work.html

Breath of Life Article about breath work, http://www.spiritbreath.com/articles/bof.html

Classic Yoga, http://www.classicyoga.org

Elements in the Practice of Yoga Types of Yoga; books, videos, CDs, http://www.yoga-for-health-and-fitness.com/yoga-basics.htm

Holistic Health and Wellness Links-Breath Work, http://www.discoverhealth andwealth.com/links/breathwork.htmlKundalini

Yoga-Links World-Wide, http://www.kundaliniyoga.org

Types of Yoga, http://www.yrec.org

Yoga Point Different Types of Yoga, http://www.yogapoint.com/info/typesof yoga.htm

Chapter 3

Success Is in the Here and Now

Stop living in a past that is gone, and a future that is yet to be. Life is only this moment, this breath, right now.

Anonymous

IN THIS CHAPTER

- Mindfulness
- Why Competing in the Here and Now Will Stop Ring Nerves
- Learning to Focus and Concentrate Under Pressure
- Staying Connected to Your Dog

> "I like to work on one thing at a time, so I didn't move on to concentration until I felt comfortable with Yoga Breath," says Jane. "The Focus on Your Body technique, coupled with the breathing, really gave me hope that I could overcome ring nerves, because if I couldn't stop my wild negative thoughts with conscious breathing—and sometimes I couldn't—then I had another tool I could pull out that would. I decided to push the envelope, and entered a number of trials in places where I had previously felt panic.
>
> "When I get to the building, I stay in the car to calm myself, then begin using Focus on Your Body as soon as I exit it. Of course, I'm quite nervous, but I use both exercises throughout the day and though we NQ'd the first time, by the second trial I felt things shifting for me. It felt so good being able to quiet myself in spite of my nerves. While waiting my turn, I combine these exercises with focusing on a point, and though initially I resisted it because I thought people would think I looked weird, it works so well that now I don't care. We placed third in the second trial! I'm still working on Focus on Your Dog. It's a hard one for me.

Sometimes I can feel her for a second, but I still can't keep that kind of mental connection going at a show. I think when I get it down, it will make a big difference in our performance and my confidence."

COMPETING IN THE MOMENT

A vital element for success in the competitive dog show world is the ability to concentrate under pressure. This skill allows your training to flow through you to your dog and into the event. It allows you to enter the "zone," that special place where mind and body, handler and dog, become one. The show environment disappears and tensions and pressures slip away. The ordinary is transformed into the extraordinary.

Competition provokes anxiety because it compares, evaluates and scores performance. This makes it difficult not only to focus, but to sustain it during an event. Many handlers who suffer from ring nerves lose concentration, which they inadvertently telegraph to their dog. This results in poor performance and low scores. Trying to focus harder doesn't change anything; in fact, it may even increase tension and anxiety.

Ring nerve symptoms are an energy drain. When mind and body are caught in anxiety's grasp, it's almost impossible to feel alert and energized. No wonder that handlers who suffer from ring nerves feel sluggish, exhausted and depleted.

Being in the present before, during and after competition helps stop negative thoughts from undermining self-esteem, eroding confidence and causing physical exhaustion. In the ring, your mind may repeat the same negative thoughts:

"I'll never be a good handler."

"We NQ'd at the last 10 shows, so what's the point in trying?"

"I keep embarrassing myself, this is ridiculous!"

If you keep listening to these negative thoughts, how will you be able to focus on your dog and do well?

The exercises in this chapter are adapted from mindfulness, meditative practices and sports psychology. They will show you how to refocus from destructive thinking onto benign objects and allow you to be present-centered. You'll become attuned to your dog during competition. With practice, these techniques will reduce anxiety and increase concentration.

In *Emotional Alchemy*, Tara Bennet-Goleman weaves together Buddhist mindfulness practice and cognitive therapy schemas. "Mindfulness," writes Bennet-Goleman, ". . . can be viewed as a systematic attempt to retain attention." One of Bennet-Goleman's teachers, Sayadaw U. Pandita, says that as we intently direct our thoughts our mind "penetrates into the object of observation moment by moment," and "gains the capacity to remain stable and undistracted, content."

Off Course

Marie competes in Agility with her Cavalier King Charles Spaniels, Winnie and Gidget. During the first few years of competition, Marie had such a bad case of nerves that she "could not focus on an entire excellent course." Fear and thoughts about their failures at previous events controlled Marie, causing her to forget the course and repeatedly take her eyes off her dog. With her ring nerves in high gear, all the time put into training her dogs didn't seem to matter, for they could not qualify.

In this chapter, you'll learn to compete in the *here and now* and to concentrate despite pressures to win. You'll be able to tune out distracting elements in the show environment. You'll be able to sense your dog, feel him, communicate with him, move with him. You'll be as one entity. Imagine how pleasurable it would be to compete with this degree of single-mindedness.

So how do you do this at a trial? How do you block out the handlers, dogs, judges and other distractions? How do you concentrate when you're being rated in front of your peers? How do you turn off negative thoughts and stop setting yourself up for failure and disappointment? What happens when you can't?

BEING IN THE HERE AND NOW

When you learn to be present or *mindful* in each moment, your ring nerves will plummet. Reliving disappointing or embarrassing past show experiences or worrying that you will repeat them will trigger your ring nerve symptoms. If you obsess about the past or future, you won't be able to concentrate on what's happening right now. You'll also find it very difficult to critique your performance and learn from your mistakes if you don't stay in the present.

Not being in the moment is being absent from life. The past is gone and the future is unknown. Right now is where it's all unfolding: the match or trial, the ring and your dog and the outcome. If you're emotionally out of it, it will be impossible to stay connected. You will never experience peak performance.

SITTING IN THE PRESENT

1. Hold this book in your lap and begin Yoga Breath for one to two minutes. Focus on your breath as it goes in and out.

2. How does it feel to hold this book? Use all your senses. What does the cover feel like? Is it smooth or rough? Look closely at the color of the cover and the typefaces used. Run your hand down the spine. Is the book heavy or light? Smell it.

Is Everyone Watching?

Paula is a professional dog trainer and competes in Obedience with her Shetland Sheepdog, Cody, and two Border Collies, Beau and Shadow. Paula always suffered from ring nerves. "It certainly has never been a thing of joy or something I truly look forward to." Paula was able to manage the pressure of competition due to the support of a large group of fellow competitors, and was consistently successful getting scores in the high 190s, and attaining her CDX with Cody. Paula's real trouble began when she changed her training methods. She left her instructor and lost the support of her group. She became concerned that "everyone," especially her old training pals, was judging her and her new methods. "I couldn't concentrate at all in the ring, and lost touch with my dog as soon as my anxiety got bad. I began to have panic attacks, and we NQ'd regularly."

3. Concentrate on the book. As random thoughts run through your mind, don't fight them. Instead, examine them and then refocus on the book in your hands.

4. Keep directing your thoughts, energy and senses on this book.

5. Now relax and think about what occurred. Were you able to fully focus on the book? Did your surroundings and your thoughts fade out even for a second? If so, how did that feel? Were you with the book in the moment?

In 1972, W. Timothy Gallwey wrote *The Inner Game of Tennis*, the groundbreaking book that illuminated the importance of the mind/body connection in all competitive undertakings. This book spawned the sport psychology movement. Gallwey's philosophy of letting go, not trying too hard, playing in the moment and learning to get out of your own way resonated with professional and amateur alike.

Gallwey wrote that learning to concentrate in the present is how to reach optimal experience. He recommended focusing on something. Gallwey used a tennis ball. You will use your body and your dog.

Try the following exercises. They will help you achieve acute attention. You'll be able to focus even in the most stressful moments. With practice, worries about the past and future will disappear.

FOCUS ON YOUR BODY

There are four exercise variations: Focus on the Chair, Eyes Closed; Focus on the Chair, Eyes Open; Focus on Your Feet, Standing; and Focus on Your Feet, Walking/Running.

Training Tip

Learning to concentrate deeply is very difficult, but very doable. Don't force it; rather, relax into each exercise and with practice it will all come together.

Focus on the Chair, Eyes Closed

1. Sit comfortably in a chair, feet flat on the floor.

2. Hands rest in your lap palms up.

3. Close your eyes.

4. Try to do Yoga Breath. If that's difficult, just breathe comfortably and easily.

5. As you sit in the chair, focus all your attention on feeling your body resting in the chair. Fix your thoughts on feeling your back against the chair and your buttocks resting on the seat.

6. Keep breathing and thinking about how it feels to sit on the chair.

7. As thoughts surface, don't fight them. Instead, allow them to be and then gently refocus on your body.

8. Keep focusing on sitting.

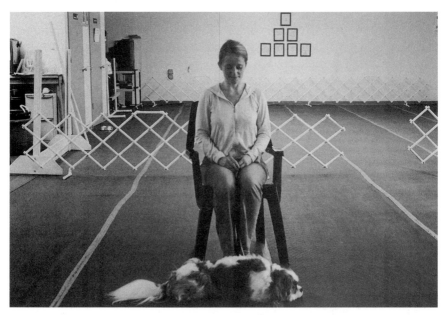

Focusing inward.

Training Tip for Sitting, Standing, Walking/Running

Set your clock or use an egg timer and begin with a minute of practice. Slowly increase time to at least five minutes per session.

9. When the time is up, relax and see how you feel.

10. Practice daily.

How did that feel? Were you able, if only for a moment, to give all of your attention to sitting?

Focus on the Chair, Eyes Open

Just as we did in Yoga Breath Eyes Open, you'll be looking at a point during this exercise to increase attention.

1. Sit comfortably in a chair, feet flat on the floor.

2. Hands rest in your lap.

3. Eyes are open.

4. Try to do Yoga Breath. If that's difficult, just breathe comfortably and easily.

5. As you sit in the chair, put all of your attention on feeling your body sitting. Focus your energy and thoughts on your back against the chair and your buttocks resting on the seat.

6. Find something in front of you to look at.

Being in the moment is calming.

7. Keep breathing and concentrate on how it feels to sit on the chair.

8. As thoughts surface, don't fight them. Instead, allow them to be and then gently refocus on your body.

9. Stay in the present.

10. When the time is up, relax and see how you feel.

11. Practice daily.

Focus on Your Feet, Standing

1. Stand tall with your shoulders and head relaxed.

2. Distribute your weight on both legs to feel balanced.

3. Begin Yoga Breath.

4. Focus on how the soles of your feet feel in your shoes and on how your feet feel on the floor while standing.

5. As thoughts surface, don't fight them. Instead, allow them to be and then gently refocus on your feet.

6. Keep feeling your feet.

7. When the time is up, relax and see how you feel.

8. Practice daily.

Shifting the focus to your feet.

Focus on Your Feet, Walking/Running

1. Stand tall with your shoulders and head relaxed.

2. Distribute your weight on both legs to feel balanced.

3. Begin Yoga Breath.

4. Focus on how the soles of your feet feel in your shoes.

5. Now begin to walk slowly, being aware of each step.

6. As thoughts surface, don't fight them. Instead, allow them to be and then gently refocus on walking.

7. Continue walking and increase the pace to running.

8. Think about how your feet feel in your shoes as you run.

9. When the time is up, relax and see how you feel.

10. Practice daily.

Did changing your pace make it hard to focus? Keep practicing!

ADVANCED PRESENT AWARENESS—PUTTING IT ALL TOGETHER

You're going to combine Sitting, Standing, Walking/Running so you can make a smooth transition from one to the other. The object is to make a quick mental shift without breaking concentration.

Sitting to Standing

1. Set the timer.

2. Sit comfortably in a chair, feet flat on the floor.

3. Hands rest in your lap.

4. Keep your eyes open.

5. Begin Yoga Breath

Training Tip for Sitting, Standing, Walking/Running

Set your clock or use an egg timer and begin with a minute of practice. Slowly increase time to 10 to 15 minutes per session. Be sure to vary the length of practice times, for example: one minute sitting, three minutes standing, five minutes walking or seven minutes sitting, two minutes standing, one minute walking, etc.

6. Put all of your attention on feeling your body resting in the chair.

7. How does it feel to sit on the chair?

8. As thoughts surface, don't fight them. Instead, allow them to be, then gently refocus on your body.

9. Keep concentrating on sitting in the chair.

10. Now, stand and immediately shift your focus to your feet.

11. Stand tall and relax your head and shoulders.

12. Distribute your weight on both legs to feel balanced.

13. Continue Yoga Breath

14. Put all of your focus on how the soles of your feet feel in your shoes.

15. How do your feet feel on the floor while you're standing?

16. As thoughts surface, don't fight them. Instead, allow them to be, then gently come back to your feet.

17. Keep feeling your feet.

18. When you are finished, relax and see how you feel.

19. Practice daily.

Sitting to Standing to Walking/Running

1. Sit comfortably in a chair, feet flat on the floor.

2. Hands rest in your lap.

3. Keep your eyes open.

4. Begin Yoga Breath

5. Put all of your attention on feeling your body resting in the chair.

6. Stand and immediately shift all of your focus onto your feet for a few seconds.

Training Tip

- When you have mastered *Focus on Your Body*, begin to include your dog in practice sessions. This is a great way to rehearse for a real show.
- Use *Focus on Your Body* in every dog training class.

7. Begin to walk, thinking of each step.

8. Make sure your body is balanced.

9. Continue Yoga Breath.

10. As thoughts surface, don't fight them. Instead, allow them to be, then gently refocus on your feet.

11. Continue walking, thinking of how it feels to walk.

12. Feel your feet in your shoes as you walk.

13. Now pick up the pace to a trot and then a run.

14. How does it feel to run?

15. When the time is up, relax and see how you feel.

16. Practice daily.

What did it feel like to keep your focus while you changed your pace?

You can find many opportunities to practice and use these techniques as you go about your daily routine.

How to Practice at Home, Work and Play

Make a conscious effort to *Focus on Your Body* throughout the day. Practice each exercise individually and in combinations.

1. Sitting eating a meal, standing to clear the table and walking to the kitchen

2. Standing in the shower

3. Sitting/standing while getting dressed

4. Walking to your vehicle

5. Sitting in your vehicle, standing outside of it and walking to a destination

6. Walking in the supermarket and standing in line

Training Tip

As it becomes easier to concentrate for longer periods, add distractions to your exercise:

- Play the radio or TV and try to block out the noise.

- Make an audio of show noises and try to tune it out.

7. Walking in your house

8. Sitting at your desk/computer and walking around at work

9. Sitting in a movie theater and walking to the candy counter

10. Sitting at a ballgame

11. Running to catch a train

12. Running through the park

13. Walking/running around with your dog

How to Use Focus on Your Body During Training Sessions and Shows

1. Walking around the house getting ready to leave

2. Standing while you put collar/harness/leash on your dog

3. Walking your dog to vehicle

4. Sitting in your vehicle on the way to class or show

5. Sitting in vehicle at show before you get out; walking/trotting into class/ show site

6. Sitting around waiting for class or event to begin

7. Running with your dog to the potty area

8. Walking/trotting/running in the ring

9. Standing in the on-deck position

10. Standing at the start

11. Walking/running entering the ring

12. Standing and walking/running in the ring

Being fully present in each moment is very difficult especially when you're under competitive pressure, but it's possible with daily practice. The benefits and rewards are well worth your time and effort.

Training Tip

Practice at each dog training session as if you and your dog were in a real show situation.

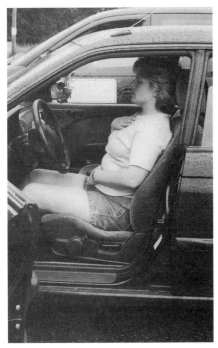

At the show, before you exit the car.

Focus in the here and now.

Focus as you touch your dog.

Maintaining focus walking to site.

Stay in the present as you
enter the building.

FOCUS ON YOUR DOG

By using a method similar to *Focus on Your Body*, the following exercises will teach you to fix your attention on your dog. Part II of *Focus on Your Dog* uses mental visualization. Since 90 percent of the sensory data that the brain receives and interprets is visual, this technique will help you impress your dog's image into your mind. Whether you're together or apart, you'll be one. *Focus on Your Dog* requires consistent practice to make it work.

Focus on Your Dog, Sitting, Part I

1. Set the timer for five minutes.

2. Sit in a comfortable chair and have your dog next to you.

3. Begin Yoga Breath.

4. Focus on your dog. Study him closely. Look at his physical details, characteristics and qualities. Open your mind to what makes your dog who he is. Look at his conformation, face, color and type of coat. What is his personality like? Is he shy? A bruiser? A goofball? What endears him to you?

5. What does he give to you emotionally? Love and happiness? Sense of responsibility? Fun and laughter? Purpose?

Staying on Course

Marie realized that she had to begin thinking and reading about her sport's mental aspects. She spotted an ad for my *Competing At Your Peak Ring Nerve Seminar*, but it was too far away, so she purchased the seminar notes (this was before the audio program was available).

"That was the missing link," Marie says. "From those notes I began teaching myself how to do Yoga Breath, Focus on Your Body, Visualization, etc. Things changed dramatically from then on, and I began to enjoy remarkable success!"

Marie has a routine that she religiously adheres to before she enters the ring. "I never go into the ring without it!" she says. One part of her routine combines Focus on Your Body with Yoga Breath. "Winnie is all excited and wild when we get ready to go to the line, then I begin my breath work and focus on my feet and watch him settle down and put all his attention on me."

How successful has Marie been?

"Since we started using the program we have progressed to competing at the highest levels of our sport, Agility. My Winnie and I have achieved AKC's highest agility title, Master Agility Champion (MACH) three times, the only Cavalier to do so and one of under 100 dogs in the country to do so. Winnie was AKC's Top Cavalier for 2000 and 2002 and the twentieth dog of all dogs in the country in double qualifications for 2002. He earned USDAA's Master Agility Dog title (MAD) and last year earned USDAA's Master Relay (RM) title. He holds UKC's Agility Champion title, his AKC Obedience CD and a couple of other accomplishments too."

6. Watch your dog closely; see and feel all of his attributes, features and idiosyncrasies. See every aspect that makes your dog who he is.

7. Now, gently stroke your dog. What does his body feel like? Is he husky or lean? Large, medium or small? What does his coat feel like? Does he have long hair or short? Is his fur smooth or rough? Stroke his ears. What do they feel like? Run your hand down his back to the end of his tail. What does his tail feel like?

8. Open all your senses to him. Bend down and let him kiss your face. Kiss him back. How does he smell? Hug your dog. How does it feel to do that?

9. Continue studying and touching your dog and imprinting all of his features, traits and characteristics into your mind and body.

10. When time is up, relax for one minute.

11. Gradually increase exercise time to 10 to 15 minutes.

Connecting with Cody.

Focus on Your Dog, Sitting, Part II

1. Set the timer for five minutes.

2. Do not touch or look at your dog.

3. Sit comfortably in your chair, feet flat on the floor, hands resting in your lap.

4. Close your eyes.

5. Begin Yoga Breath.

6. See your dog clearly in your mind's eye. Try to pull up the mental imprint of your dog from Part I. See and feel his every characteristic, attribute and feature as if you were looking at and stroking him.

7. Do not force this image to appear, just breathe and relax and let the image of your dog float to the surface of your mind.

Training Tip

When you want to quickly connect with your dog, add a cue. When you practice *Focus on Your Dog*, tap part of your body when your dog's image surfaces, so that at a show a tap means your dog's image with feelings of connection.

Training Tip

- Practice *Focus on Your Dog* daily and in time you'll see a great increase in your ability to stay connected to him in any circumstance.

- Slowly increase practice time until you can concentrate without too much distraction for at least 10 minutes.

8. If you become distracted, gently refocus on your dog's image.

9. Imagine that with invisible hands, you reach out to embrace him and bring him to you. Imagine you can feel all of the physical aspects of your dog's body.

10. Totally relax and open your senses, keeping yourself free and flowing in the experience of uniting with the image of your dog until you feel you are one entity.

11. Continue until time is up.

12. Relax and see how you feel.

13. Practice daily.

What was this experience like for you? How often were you distracted by other thoughts? Did you feel yourself bond with the image of your dog?

Focus on Your Dog, Standing

Before you proceed, make sure you can invoke your dog's image quickly and can feel the connection and hold it for a few minutes.

1. Set the timer for five minutes.

2. Sit in a chair with your dog next to you.

Training Tip

- Practice at every training session.
- Practice Focus on Your Body and Focus on Your Dog together.

3. Begin Yoga Breath.

4. For about 30 seconds, focus all of your attention onto your dog and then gently stroke him.

5. Continue studying and touching your dog. Imprint his features, traits and characteristics for another 30 seconds.

6. Now stand up with your dog beside you and make that mental connection with him. Although you're not touching him, you should feel yourself united with him. He is part of you and you are part of him.

7. Continue feeling how your dog is imprinted in your psyche.

8. When time is up, relax for one minute.

9. Gradually increase practice time to 10 to 15 minutes.

10. Practice daily.

Focus on Your Dog, Walking/Running

1. Set the timer for five to 10 minutes.

2. Stand with your dog at your side.

3. Bring up your dog's image and your feelings of being connected to him.

4. Begin Yoga Breath.

5. Begin walking with him at your side and feel his presence.

6. Vary your pace to simulate your event. Try to keep the connection.

7. When time is up, sit and relax.

8. Increase practice time to 15 minutes.

9. Practice daily.

Now that you've practiced for a little while, is the connection easier to keep?

Training Tip

Practice three to four times a day for three weeks, conjuring up the image of your dog when you are apart from her, then see how much more connected you are at your next competition.

Focusing on Cody

Paula also combined Yoga Breath with *Focus on Your Body* and *Focus on Your Dog* with great results. At her last show, Paula felt highly stressed and began to have negative thoughts about herself during her event. She started Yoga Breath and used *Focus on Your Feet* with *Focus on Your Dog*. "I was able to work through the emotions even while in the ring! Normally, I disconnect from my dog as soon as my anxiety spikes, but this time I felt we had an invisible string attached to us and I could get him back to me if I tuned out. It made me feel powerful that I could change those destructive thoughts I have and settle myself down. I'm actually looking forward to my next show!" Paula and Cody got their ASCA CD title.

COMBINING METHODS

As you practice *Focus on Your Body* and *Focus on Your Dog* and are able to stay in the *here and now* for longer periods of time, you will feel the apprehension of competition slip away. Negative thoughts will lose their power. You'll be alert and feel energized. You'll be with your dog all the way. You'll connect with your performance both physically and mentally. You'll feel more alive. You may even begin to enjoy competition!

Add the exercises in this chapter into your daily training program and practice whenever and wherever you can. In time, you'll feel the powerful difference they will make in competition as well as in other aspects of life, for both you and your dog.

FURTHER READING

Tara Bennett-Goleman. *Emotional Alchemy.* Harmony Books, 2001.

Ram Dass. *Be Here Now.* Crown, 1971.

Shannon Duncan. *Present Moment Awareness: A Simple Step-By-Step Guide to Living in the Now.* New World Library, 2003.

Mark Epstein, M.D. *Going On Being.* Broadway Books New York, 2001.

Thich Nhat Hanh. *Our Appointment With Life: The Buddhas Teaching on Living in the Present.* Parallax, 1990.

Leonard Jacobson. *Embracing the Present.* Conscious Living Publications, 1997.

Eckhart Tolle. *The Power of Now.* New World Library, 1999.

RESOURCE LIST

Center for Transformational Psychotherapy: Living in the Moment, http://www.forhealing.org/inthemoment.html

Living in the Moment, http://angelreiki.nu/reiki-do/moment.htm

Living in the Moment Online Magazine, http://www.taichiacademy.com.au/magazine/feature13.htm

Living in the Present, http://www.livinginthepresent.com

Living in the Present, http:// www.successconsciousness.com

Mindfulness and Being Present, http://www.soulfulliving.com

Naka-Ima: Living in the Present, http://www.lostvalley.org/naka-ima.html

Tao Living. Living in the Moment, http://www.taoism.net/living/200301.htm

What's Important Now?, http://www.presentliving.org/e-thoughts.htm

Chapter 4

Go With the Flow!

You gain strength, courage and confidence by every experience in which you really stop and look fear in the face.
Eleanor Roosevelt

IN THIS CHAPTER

- Fighting Against Ring Nerves Will Only Heighten Them
- Facing Your Feared Experiences Will Render Them Powerless
- Stop Being Afraid of Being Afraid
- Learning to Go With the Flow
- Avoidance

"Go With the Flow was hard to learn," says Jane. "I had Yoga Breath and Focus on Your Body down pat, but when I started practicing, I knew it would take me time to get the hang of it. As Diane says, an internal shift has to take place, and that takes time. It was terrible for me at first; my body wouldn't give up the fight, so I visualized myself gently floating on the crest of a giant wave with an ocean full of competition fears churning beneath me. It was quiet and calm on the crest, and I learned to let the storm of fear swirl under and around me, and could float on my back and watch it and see that it couldn't touch me. I visualize that I'm floating into a calm sea, and that helps to quiet my mind. The best part is that I'm slowly beginning to believe I can do anything I want to do now, like compete in Agility or Obedience. When the sea of ring nerves is roiling, and I really let go and accept, my anxiety nosedives."

FIGHTING YOUR FEARS

Powerful physical changes occur when you feel threatened in a competition. Stress hormones flood your body, tensing it for fight or flight. Symptoms of anxiety appear, such as pounding heart, stiffness and shaking limbs. Your breathing becomes rapid and shallow or you may even hold your breath, which escalates anxiety while the mind races with thoughts of impending disaster. As tension builds, all logic and reasoning shuts down and emotions take over. You're filled with overwhelming feelings of loss of control and helplessness.

It's instinctive to fight the fear. You shut down both mind and body with extreme tension. The intense sensations associated with ring nerves can make competing feel like a life-or-death struggle. If you seize up, you may feel as if you're controlling your nerves, but you're not. You're just frozen solid, unable to move forward toward achievement and fulfillment as a competitor.

If you try to keep every uncomfortable thought and emotion locked away, as Marion did (see *Panic Attack*), then you'll have to block out everything, including your dog and the event. By shutting down to cope with nerves, you're leaving your dog alone without a teammate.

Defending against fear and trying to calm yourself by "white knuckling" it will never make ring nerves go away. This strategy will only worsen them and make it impossible for you to give a good performance. In addition, you'll never experience the pleasure of the sport you love so much if you shut down.

In *Awakening the Heart* (New Science Library, 1985), John Welwood writes, "Reacting against emotions—fearing our fear, being angry about our anger, getting depressed about our sadness—is much worse than these primary feelings themselves, for it freezes them and turns us against ourselves."

WHAT CAN YOU DO?

But what can you do against ring nerves? Stop fighting against or trying to bury ring nerves' frightening physical and mental manifestations. Ride out the storm by relaxing into distressful thoughts and painful feelings, yet stay

Panic Attack

"I've always been shy and a little anxious," Marion says. "I wanted very much to compete in Obedience and Rally-O, even though the thought of it scared me. When I actually started showing things got really bad for me. I just shook all over right before my turn, couldn't concentrate at all and felt panicky from the time I got there until I was on my way home. I was terrified that I'd have a full blown panic attack, so I'd clench my jaw and grind my teeth to keep my fear in check. My jaw and body were so rigid in the ring that they actually hurt for hours after.

Handlers in my class told me to "just go in and have fun," but I couldn't. I had a friend videotape my performance because we NQ'd all the time, and I could never remember a thing about our event. I tried to watch the tape, but it made me feel worse, so I turned it off and haven't been able to look at it since."

connected to them. It's all about not being afraid of being afraid. Sounds tough to do, right? It is! But with determination and practice, being able to *go with the flow* will loosen the powerful grip of ring nerves and change negative competition experiences into positive ones.

MORE THAN RELAXATION

Relaxation certainly plays a large part in mastering how to accept your fears, but Go With the Flow is a technique with much deeper significance. We're after a change in the psyche at the very heart of your mind and body. If you truly believe that the symptoms of ring nerves cannot harm you, they won't have control over you. As Dr. Claire Weekes writes in *More Help for Your Nerves* (Bantam Books, 1987), "The true cure will come when . . . it doesn't matter if it [panic] does happen here."

Dr Weekes, an Australian physician, pioneered methods to cure anxiety, agoraphobia and panic. Her treatments were so successful that she was nominated for the Nobel Prize for Medicine in 1989. Several of her books are still in print thirty years later. Dr Weekes believed that severe anxiety could develop from "stress and nervous fatigue to produce a pattern of symptoms which can become more frightening than the original cause."

Weekes's recovery program includes:

1. *Facing*: Acknowledge that you are afraid, that the remedy comes ultimately from you, and that you must not avoid "the places and experiences feared."
2. *Accepting*: When panic hits, loosen your body as much as possible to reduce tension and anxiety and continue with what you are doing.
3. *Floating*: Relax into the panic instead of fighting against it.
4. *Letting Time Pass*: Recovery takes time; there is "no overnight cure."

Welwood writes that the common experience of handling emotions on a daily basis is that they are beyond our control, making them "confusing and frightening. " But if we "befriend emotions in a more direct and fearless way, [and] . . . go deeply into them, go toward them, face them as they are, then [we] can allow their energies to expand our sense of what we are." When we connect to our emotional being, though it can be uncomfortable, it enables us to bond more fully with life. It allows us to face and deal with whatever life has to offer, including all circumstances in the dog show arena.

DON'T JUST MANAGE THE FEAR

You can control ring nerves, but they will continue to resurface if you fail to lose your fear of being afraid. In Annie's case, (see *Ring Nerves Resurface*), Annie believed she had licked ring nerves, and she thought they would never return. She contacted me again, this time saying that she'd never free herself

Ring Nerves Resurface

Annie got into competing like most handlers. She fell in love with a cute little Sheltie named Tommy. Annie took Tommy to training class and loved working with him. Initially, she was thrilled with the idea of showing in competition obedience.

Annie was surprised how anxious she felt in their first show. By the second show she was already developing a case of ring nerves. About 18 months later, Annie decided to quit because her symptoms had become unbearable. They couldn't qualify, and Tommy, who was tuned into her nerves, began reacting negatively each time they entered the ring.

Annie's last-ditch effort was to attend a Ring Nerve Seminar. For months after, she diligently practiced the techniques and exercises, until she felt confident enough to begin to enter shows again. The more Annie used what she learned, the better they did. Tommy earned his CD and when he qualified, it was always in the top four places. He had a wall of blue, red, yellow and white ribbons, and her ring nerves seemed to be a thing of the past.

A little over a year later, Annie decided to try Agility. She was no longer practicing the exercises regularly, only using them if her nerves surfaced during a show. At first things went smoothly, Tommy got his NAJ, but suddenly, Annie's ring nerves returned at an Agility trial. This time they were so severe that she felt devastated and completely hopeless.

From then on, Agility was something to be feared.

"It has been so bad of late that I've actually gotten up to the starting line and considered backing out of the event. I'm often so lightheaded that I'm afraid I'm going to faint, or my legs are so shaky that I can't keep up with Tommy in the ring. One time he did a perfect run up until about the last five jumps, but I was so exhausted from preshow anxiety that I couldn't run the last jumps with him and he quit on me. Lately it's become painful in a physical and emotional sense, and he's doing less well at each trial. When he doesn't "Q" I feel like such a failure and the disappointment is shattering."

from ring nerves and that she was thinking about quitting Agility. She was now also worrying at Obedience trials, fearing ring nerves would strike there, too.

Annie never lost her fear of being afraid. Yes, she had tools from the Ring Nerve Seminar to help her feel more relaxed and to build confidence, but Annie had only learned how to manage, control and bury her feelings. When the old symptoms returned, her immediate reaction was to tense up and fight them, which only exacerbated the situation.

Annie is now practicing the seminar techniques that she learned in the past and has added Go With the Flow to her training program. From now on, ring nerves may appear, but she'll never be surprised again or let it keep her from competition.

In *Awakening the Heart*, Welwood writes that in our Western culture emotions are treated and expressed as "separate from us." When we face and connect fully with them, we recognize their living energy. Instead of burying this source of power, we can use it to live out our passions.

The exercises that follow will train you to stop defending yourself from ring nerves. You'll learn to surrender to your uncomfortable feelings so that you can funnel that energy into your performance.

FACING RING NERVES

Acknowledge that you experience ring nerves. This may be quite distressing and painful. It is very difficult to look our fears squarely in the eye and admit that they wield so much power. We often perceive these sensations as being dangerous and harmful, but although we feel they can hurt us, they can't. Facing our fear head-on is the most important step to overcoming it.

Exercise

1. Use this guide to create your *feared scene* on the form below. Write down the details of a show you attended where you experienced ring nerves, or write the details of an imaginary situation such as one you fear may happen. Be sure to include your feelings and reactions, what occurred or what

---

Ring Nerve Anxiety Scale

10_____ Panic city!!!

9_____ How do I get off this runaway train?!

8_____ No place to run, no place to hide

7_____ They're he-e-ere!

6_____ Not feeling so hot

5_____ Feel the build

4_____ Uh-oh!

3_____ First twinges

2_____ So far so good

1_____ Feelin' pretty cool

0_____ No ring nerves in sight

Note: You may photocopy this form if you wish.

you fear will occur and your dog's response. Include training class and preshow preparation time. Use the information from the exercise at the end of Chapter One to help you.

2. Rate each aspect of your visualization using the following Ring Nerve Anxiety Scale. For example:

   - I think about getting lost on the way to a show site I've never been to before: 7

   - During the last trial, I was afraid I'd faint in the on-deck position: 9

   - I'm terrified my dog will humiliate me by running around the ring: 10

3. Continue filling in levels of anxiety for each component of your feared scene.

4. When you finish, relax with Yoga Breath for a few minutes.

5. Read over what you've written trying to feel and stay with each moment of your feared scene as if it were happening now.

Construct Your Feared Scene: Real or Imagined

Competition event(s) _____

Training class and/or preshow preparations: _____

_____

_____

_____

_____

At the show: _____

_____

_____

_____

_____

On deck: _____

_____

_____

_____

_____

In the ring: _____

_____

_____

_____

_____

_____

After or in between shows: _____

_____

_____

_____

_____

_____

Construct Your Feared Scene: Real or Imagined Sample

Here is Marion's feared scene. She plays this one constantly every time she enters a show.

Competition event: *Obedience*

Training class and/or pre-show preparations: *I know how acutely embarrassed I am because I'm shaking in my boots, and have to face other handlers in my class after a show. 8. Days before the show I'm so jumpy and my stomach acts up. I have diarrhea and live on Imodium. 7*

At the show: *I really obsess that I won't hear my number, so I'm anxious that I'll miss my turn and look stupid. I get frantic and I'm on deck way too soon. 8*

On deck: *I see myself having to scratch because my panic is building, I get lightheaded and think everyone will notice. 9*

In the ring: *I'm so rigid, so shut down that I mentally blank out. Sometimes when my nerves are really bad, I can't see or hear clearly. I'm afraid of having a panic attack and looking like I'm going crazy. 10. I'm terrified that my dog will embarrass me. 10*

After or in between shows: *I worry all the time about how I'm going to stop my anxiety from happening the next time. 6 to 7*

LET GO AND ACCEPT

In this section, you'll learn how to release mind/body tensions and accept all of the feared physical and mental symptoms when you dive into a feared scene.

Training Tip

You may have other feared scenes, so practice with those as well.

You're going to practice riding the wave of distressing emotions by not fighting and blocking, but by totally relaxing and yielding to them.

In *Working Out, Working Within* (Jeremy P. Tarcher/Putnam, 1999), Jerry Lynch writes about facing fear. "The Tao encourages against fighting or forcing away fear as this will create inner turmoil, tension and anxiety, all of which interfere with performance of any kind."

Letting Go, Sitting or Prone Position

1. Set the timer for three to five minutes.

2. Sit in a comfortable chair, feet flat on the floor, hands in your lap. Or lie down, hands resting at your sides, legs slightly apart.

3. Relax your head, neck and shoulders.

4. Eyes are open or closed.

5. Now, either read your notes or envision your feared scene and try to induce feelings of anxiety.

6. Begin doing Yoga Breath and as soon as you feel uneasy or apprehensive don't fight these feelings. Instead, allow them to come to the surface.

7. As you look at your feared scene, let all of the emotions and thoughts come right at you. Don't panic or fight. You're safe and you're going to relax. Don't hold your breath.

8. Feel your whole body floating on the crest of emotion, knowing nothing can harm you. Stay calm in body and mind and keep your breath slow, smooth and quiet.

9. Let your feelings come! Breathe into them.

10. Try not to tense yourself.

11. When time is up, relax and see how you feel.

12. For optimum results, practice daily.

Were you able to Go With the Flow for a few seconds or at all? This is one of the most difficult techniques to learn. Freeing yourself from fear is hard to do because an internal emotional shift has to take place, which takes time and many hours of practice to learn. But the payoff is well worth the effort!

Training Tip

If you struggle with Yoga Breath, review Chapter Two and practice the breathing again before continuing with this chapter.

Letting Go, Standing

1. Set the timer for three to five minutes.
2. Stand tall, head and shoulders relaxed.
3. Distribute your weight on both legs to feel balanced.
4. Eyes are open.
5. Concentrate on relieving all the tension in your head, neck and shoulders.
6. Relax your torso, arms, hands, lower body, legs and feet.
7. Allow your body to go slack.
8. Now, visualize your feared scene and invite the anxiety to surface.
9. Your gut reaction will be to tense up, but don't give in to that. Instead begin Yoga Breath. Breathe into it, keeping your mind and body as calm as possible.
10. Let whatever feelings and thoughts emerge. They can't harm you.
11. Continue to breathe and keep your body as loose and relaxed as possible.
12. As you learn to Go With the Flow, the power of ring nerves will lessen.
13. When time is up, see how you feel.
14. Practice daily.

Be proud of your achievement of trying to face your fears. The effort is the real victory.

Letting Go, Walking/Running

1. Set the timer for three to five minutes.
2. Stand tall, head and shoulders relaxed.
3. Distribute your weight on both legs to feel balanced.
4. Start walking slowly.
5. Now, picture your feared scene and let all the feelings and thoughts associated with it surface.
6. At the same time, begin Yoga Breath and let your body go limp.

Training Tip

If you find it difficult to go slack on command, think of yourself as a Raggedy Ann or Andy doll or imagine what it would feel like being a strand of overcooked spaghetti.

7. Try not to battle your fear, but submit to it. Do Yoga Breath and continue to relax.

8. As you walk, continue breathing. Release all of the tension in mind and body. Keep walking, facing your fears.

9. By relaxing into and accepting all the anxiety you have about yourself, you'll render ring nerves harmless. They're no longer able to block your success and happiness.

10. Change the pace to trotting or running and continue to breathe and let go.

11. When time is up, sit down, relax and meditate on what occurred and how you feel about it.

12. Practice Go With the Flow daily.

ADD CALMING STATEMENTS

As you practice Go With the Flow, you may want to add comforting statements to quiet and relax your mind and to counteract your negative mental tapes. Following are some sample phrases to use or you may use your own.

Soothing Phrases

- I'm anxious, but my feelings can't hurt me.
- I'm letting my body move into my fear and panic and nothing will happen.
- I'm at a dog show, and I'm at peace.
- I'm calming myself so that my dog will feel calm.

Training Tip

While practicing variations of *Go With the Flow,* include your dog.

Going With The Flow

Marion included Go With the Flow in her training program. "It was scary at first," she says, "and I started practicing in the prone position, because it was easier to relax that way. When you spend a lifetime pushing this stuff away, it's awfully hard to command your mind not to react. The breathing and concentration exercises helped, but sometimes I was so afraid weeks before a show that no exercise could touch it. I thought a lot about what I was afraid of, and I think it's that anxiety will build up so much and turn into a panic attack. I had panic attacks years ago before I started competing and I've had it under control for a long time.

"It took me days to remember all the details of past shows because I feel shame that I never do well, so I block it all out. Labeling the levels of fear helps to create a distance between me and my anxiety. Trying to accept that this is how I feel, but that I'm changing things, makes me feel more in control. Part Two, Letting Go, was hard to do. I started with the first thing on my list, which was mailing in my premium for a trial. I set the timer for about 30 seconds, because that's all I thought I could tolerate. But every day for weeks after, I worked on my feared scene a little bit at a time, and slowly things began to change. I could think about competing without the usual tension. I began to practice at work too, especially when I had to attend meetings, which usually made me very tense, and I found my anxiety slowly lessening.

"The best thing is, I've been using Go With the Flow for almost a year now, and because I really believe that my fear can't hurt me, I'm relaxing much more, and we have two legs on our CD. I'm still nervous, and once in a while I feel out of control, but now I handle ring nerves so much better."

When and Where to Practice

1. At home, before leaving for a training class or show picture your feared scene or let what you're presently worrying about surface

2. In your vehicle, before class or a show

3. Right before you touch your dog to take him out of the vehicle

4. Walking your dog to the show site

5. Getting your number and setting up

6. Waiting for your turn

7. Standing in the on-deck position

8. Standing at the start

> **Training Tip**
>
> Begin all *calming statements* with "I," and make them meaningful.

9. In the ring

10. After the show when you assess your performance

Be patient and gentle with yourself as you learn Go with the Flow. These exercises are hard for everyone to master because the change involves an internal process. It takes hours of repetition.

AVOIDANCE

It is natural for people who experience overwhelming anxiety to avoid uncomfortable situations. Avoidance is a great defense for keeping distressing emotions at bay, but it puts a major kink in living a proactive life. Sometimes we are aware of what we avoid, but often it's an unconscious process. We find justification for not participating in order to protect ourselves.

Avoidance curtails the freedom to make choices and achieve goals. It can crush your dreams as a dog handler. Facing what you avoid and why and accepting that you do so is a major step in freeing yourself from ring nerves. Add overcoming avoidant behavior to your training program.

The following exercise exposes the people, places and experiences that you avoid. Read the examples and see if any apply. Be honest with yourself beyond the obvious to see if you can add to the list below.

What are you avoiding and why?

- Pushing myself further in training, because I'm afraid to fail and feel humiliated

- Getting to the next level in my sport because I'm afraid to succeed and face the responsibility, opportunity and changes it will bring

> **Training Tip**
>
> Practice all variations of Go With the Flow in situations that arouse unease or anxiety, wherever that may be. Use at home, work or play to keep you generally relaxed and to learn to let go on command.

> **Training Tip**
>
> Tape Go with the Flow exercises for easy practicing and use before and at shows.

- Entering certain shows because I'm afraid that I can't measure up to other handlers
- Changing training schools because I don't want my instructor to get angry at me

Prepare to Face Avoidance

1. Sit in a comfortable chair, feet flat on the floor.

2. Relax your head, neck and shoulders.

3. Begin Yoga Breath.

4. Open to what, how and why you might avoid certain places, situations or people. Don't force it; just breathe, think and write it all down.

5. Rate each avoidant behavior on the Ring Nerve Avoidance Scale below.

Avoidant Behavior Exercise

1. I avoid _____

   _____

   Because _____

   _____

   Ring Nerve Avoidance Scale rating _____

   _____

2. I avoid _____

   _____

   _____

   Because _____

   _____

   _____

   Ring Nerve Avoidance Scale rating _____

   _____

3. I avoid _____

_____

_____

Because _____

_____

Ring Nerve Avoidance Scale rating _____

_____

_____

4. I avoid _____

_____

_____

Because _____

_____

_____

Ring Nerve Avoidance Scale rating _____

_____

Add any additional avoidant behaviors to your Ring Nerve Journal.

When you're finished, read over what you've written and congratulate yourself on facing yet another aspect of your fears. Was it tough to do this exercise? Did you get new insights into what might be blocking your success? If you've struggled to come up with anything that you avoid, repeat the exercise as needed, making sure you're as relaxed and open as possible. You can now take steps toward changing these behaviors, or use this information when we tackle self-esteem and assertiveness in the next chapter.

Jane's Progress

Let's look at Jane again. Jane knew she was very avoidant and listed some of the situations she was evading because they would bring her discomfort.

Jane's Avoidant Behavior Exercise

1. **I avoid** *speaking to my friend who takes dog training classes with me and jokes about my nerves in front of other handlers.*

   Because *I hate confrontation and don't want her to feel hurt or get angry at me.*

   Ring Nerve Avoidance Scale rating 9

Ring Nerve Avoidance Scale

10_____ I'm out of here!!

9_____ How do I get off this runaway train?!

8_____ High anxiety!!

7_____ They're he-e-ere!

6_____ SOS

5_____ Feel the build

4_____ Troubled waters

3_____ First twinges

2_____ I'm cool

1_____ Feelin' pretty cool

0_____ Can face anything

2. I avoid *attending all my classes.*

   Because *my anxiety is popping up there too.*

   Ring Nerve Avoidance Scale rating 8

3. I avoid *making a decision to quit competing, at least for a while.*

   Because *of how it will look to others, and I'll feel like a complete failure.*

   Ring Nerve Avoidance Scale 6

Jane says, "It took a lot of hard work to face that I was trying to escape so much of my life, but I worked on making small changes. I stopped going to class, which was very hard to do, but what a relief, even though I felt awful about it at first. Soon after that I began weekly low-key training with another friend of mine in her backyard, and made the decision to stop competing until I got back on track."

Learning to accept fear and not fight it and to explore how and why you avoid certain situations can be a complex, strenuous and sometimes painful lesson. But since working through fear is an essential element in overcoming ring nerves, you'll want to make the effort to work on the material included in this chapter and add it to your daily training program. Believe in yourself. You're now on the road to freedom from ring nerves. You will do it!

FURTHER READING

Pema Chodron and Emily Hillburn. *Feel Comfortable With Uncertainty: 108 Teachings.* Shambhala Publications, 2002.

Pema Chodron. *The Places That Scare You: A Guide to Fearlessness in Difficult Times.* Shambhala Publications, 2001.

Mihaly Csikszentmihalyi. *Flow: The Psychology of Optimal Experience.* HarperCollins, 1993.

W. Timothy Gallwey. *The Inner Game of Tennis* (revised edition). Random House, 1997.

Susan Jackson and Mihaly Csikszentmihalyi. *Flow In Sports.* Human Kinetics, 1999.

Claire Weekes. *Hope and Help for Your Nerves.* Signet, 1991.

Claire Weekes. *More Help For Your Nerves.* Bantam Books, 1987.

Claire Weekes. *Peace From Nervous Suffering.* Signet, 1990.

John Welwood, ed. *Awakening the Heart.* New Science Library, 1983.

RESOURCE LIST

Anxiety Disorders Association of Victoria, http://www.adavic.org

CyberPsych-Anxiety Disorders Book Store, http://www.cyberpsych.org/anxbook.htm

Dr. Claire Weekes, http://www.talkingbooks.org

From Fear Into Love (InnerSelf.com), http://www.innerself.com/Meditation/weekly/from_fear_to_love.htm

Panic Disorder Resources, http://www.mental-health-matters.com/disorders/dis_resources.php?disID=69

Chapter 5

Creating a Safe Space

If you imagine it, you can achieve it. If you can dream it, you can become it.

Wm. Archer Ward

IN THIS CHAPTER

- Visualization: A Mind/Body Technique
- Creating a Mental Shelter
- Grounding Yourself in the Ring
- A Cloaking Device

> "I'm a very visual person, so the images really help when my fear begins," says Jane. "My Blue Skies is being home with Goldie, sitting on the porch, me on the wicker rocker, Goldie curled up on the settee. When we began to compete again, I was terrified at first and could barely get through the door of the site. Blue Skies was my cue to take me back to my porch, and my anxiety would ease up a little and I could go in. When I practice I touch a pin that I always wear while competing; it has become my touchstone. When I feel like I'm falling apart, having physical contact with the pin makes it easier for my Blue Skies to appear.
>
> "I made my Beam a tree with deep roots that keep my safely on the ground. When I'm very nervous, I feel like I'm literally coming out of my body, and my footwork gets sloppy and I feel clumsy. This image of the tree with roots helps keep me balanced.
>
> "I love the Bubble. Being invisible in it stops me from feeling so vulnerable when I compete. I work hard to keep the Bubble around me throughout my event."

Judging Yourself

"The thing I feel most sensitive about when I go into the ring is being judged," says Lisa. "Since I've been in the sport a long time, working my way up to be a teacher and now qualified to judge, I feel as though I should be doing better (the inner judge), and that others think that, too (judged by others). Someone said to me the other day that we are cursed in our culture by the saying, 'Those who can, do; those who can't, teach.' It's true for me that this statement is deadly, though I've always known that teaching Agility and competing in it are two different skills, but I carry that notion. I am too caught up in wanting certain results during competition, then when I can't get them, I'm prone to think that I really don't know what I'm doing, and if I fail enough, "they'll" finally see that it's true. So I'm always in danger when I'm out there, feeling exposed and vulnerable. My skill has grown, but my inner voice is more negative than ever about not knowing what I'm doing. I do so want to enjoy competition the same way I enjoy the good times with the dogs at home, but see that my difficulties in competition have also tainted some of the times at home. I'm always carrying around this terrible sense of dread, that something bad is going to happen to me. It's crazy, I tell myself, this is only an Agility trial, but that's how I feel."

VISUALIZE YOUR RING NERVES AWAY

Lisa's story (see *Judging Yourself*) details major characteristics of ring nerves: feeling exposed, being easily shaken and feeling defenseless and vulnerable.

One effective technique used by athletes, actors and others to overcome performance anxiety is visualization. It creates a mental oasis and is a source of energy to draw on when the going gets tough. In a later chapter, we'll use visualization to rehearse your perfect performance, but for now we'll focus on turning off anxiety.

VISUALIZATION

The positive or negative images you carry into the ring will influence the outcome of your performance. What you think, believe and feel about yourself surfaces where you're going to be evaluated before your co-competitors. Since our bodies cannot distinguish between responses to real events or ones that we imagine, the kind of a handler you believe you are becomes your reality. If you think you're lousy compared to others, your performance and scores will show it. Your body reacts to these thoughts with muscle and facial tension. How you handle your dog in the ring will differ from how you work with him in training class.

We can use direct conscious visualization as a potent weapon in combating ring nerves. Studies have shown that our thoughts influence our entire physiological state. Think back to or imagine a humiliating incident befalling you in the ring. Your body geared up its defenses and left you trembling, out of control and panicky. If this negative experience can make such an impact on your body, imagine what positive thoughts can do.

In this chapter, you'll learn three visualizations to help you feel grounded, secure and centered. *Blue Skies* is a safe mental shelter filled with elements that will help keep you on course during competition. The *Beam*, an intersection of two rays of warmth and power, forms an axis of strength at your core. And the *Bubble* is a cloaking device that will make you feel invisible and protected, as if you're safely training by yourself in your own backyard.

BLUE SKIES

Mike Bailey, a former Olympic Decathlete who is now a professional coach and personal trainer, says that the importance of mental preparation to handle performance anxiety in any competitive endeavor can't be emphasized enough. His story gave me the name for *Blue Skies*.

"It doesn't matter how well physically trained you are," Mike says, "if your emotions get out of hand, you're lost, whether you're competing in an Olympic trial or an Agility trial. I spent a long time making sure that even if my body felt like it was breaking down while I was racing, my mind would get me through. I used to be a basket case before competition, but my coach made me work on my mental state and I created an image that would not only relax me, but allow me to pull energy reserves from, because fear can just zap you with fatigue.

"My *thinking place* was something I love: the beach, the ocean and beautiful blue skies. I trained myself so well mentally that after a while all I needed to think was *Blue Skies* and no matter what was happening and where I was in the race that put me back in the mental state to perform at my peak. There have been times when I was way behind in some events and just wracked with nerves and physical pain, but when I opened to Blue Skies, I was often able to win or at least reach a personal best."

Forming and shaping this special place in your mind and filling it with elements that you can access quickly to make you feel sheltered will require imagination, openness and hard work.

Tips for Creating Visualizations

1. Make your images personal and meaningful to give them the power to instantly override your feared scene.

2. Create a cue word or a short phrase, like "Mike's Blue Skies," for easy access to your visualization when your anxiety is in high gear.

Training Tip

If it's difficult for you to create an image, pick the first thing that comes to mind, even if you can't attach much feeling to it. As you practice and use this exercise, your positive image should still work as a powerful cue to cope well when you feel anxious.

Creating Blue Skies

1. Sit in a chair, feet flat on the floor and hands resting in your lap. Or lie down, hands resting at your sides, legs relaxed.

2. Have your notebook nearby or use the form at the end of this exercise.

3. Do Yoga Breath for two to three minutes and continue it for this exercise.

4. Close your eyes.

5. Picture yourself and your dog either with someone, at some place or doing something that invokes feelings of safety. Make the images detailed. For example: white clouds, calm seas, green mountains, your best friend's face. You want these images to have deep emotional significance, so you can call upon them quickly in difficult situations.

6. Continue breathing and see all the details of your Blue Skies.

7. Sit, breathe and imprint the image of this secure, comfortable space in your mind. Whatever you need for your event, for your dog and for your-self to deal with the day is in this quiet and reliable space that you have created.

8. Add as many details to your space as possible to make it substantial and come alive.

9. Write down all the details of your Blue Skies.

The Blue Skies Form

1. My Blue Skies image looks like: _____

_____

_____

_____

_____

2. **My Blue Skies image is filled with:** _____

_____

_____

_____

_____

_____

3. **My Blue Skies cue word or phrase is:** _____

_____

4. **I can use Blue Skies in the following circumstances:** _____

_____

_____

_____

_____

_____

Examples of Blue Skies

Here are several Blue Skies that handlers have constructed:

Handler #1

"As soon as I closed my eyes and thought of feeling safe at a show, my best friend, who's very supportive, popped into my mind. I saw her standing right next to me, and the vision of her was so strong, I could actually feel her presence and hear her saying, 'Go out there, I know you can do it!' I take her image along with me to every show."

Handler #2

"It's always the ocean. I see myself walking along the beach at the water's edge with my dogs next to me. Throughout my life, the sound of waves breaking on the beach has always been calming for me. It's peaceful and quiet and I can feel the warmth of the sun. This will definitely work for me at trials."

Handler #3

"I see myself at home with my dog, and we're practicing in the yard where I feel safe. We're training but we're also having fun and I feel very connected, incredibly energized and we're at the top of our game, and everything flows perfectly."

Example of a Blue Skies Form

Following is Lisa's Blue Skies form:

1. **My Blue Skies image looks like**: *me with the dogs on my farm, playing around the Agility course set up in the yard. There's no pressure, and I'm having fun working with them because I love being with and training them. The air is crisp and clear, and it's quiet and peaceful.*

2. **My Blue Skies image is filled with:** *love for my dogs and good relaxed fun, and feelings of tranquility. It's also a receptacle filled with strength and confidence.*

3. **My Blue Skies cue word or phrase is**: *farm*

4. **I can use Blue Skies in the following circumstances:** *In the waiting area and at the start; when my inner criticisms begin, and my body freezes; when the dogs make mistakes and my own powerlessness overwhelms me; and definitely for strength when fatigue hits.*

Blue Skies, Prone Position or Sitting, Eyes Closed

1. Set the timer for 10 minutes

2. Sit in a chair, feet flat on the floor and hands resting in your lap. Or lie down, hands resting at your sides, legs relaxed.

3. Close your eyes.

4. Picture your feared scene (see Chapter 4).

5. Try putting yourself in this feared scene, feeling all the anxieties you have about competing and about yourself as a handler. Try not to block the anxiety. Get yourself as worked up as possible. Feel all the details of this uncomfortable experience.

6. Begin Yoga Breath and at the same time shift your mental picture to your Blue Skies image, feeling how secure and protected and invincible you are.

7. Continue bringing up your feared scene and then quickly change it into your Blue Skies experience. Accompany with Yoga Breath.

Training Tip

Blue Skies can become a quick mental and emotional switch. It will be hard to do it at first, but don't force it, just relax and breathe yourself right into your Blue Skies experience.

Training Tip

A good time to practice is in bed right before you go to sleep. When you're tired and your defenses are down, your feared scene may create heightened ring nerve sensations, adding an edge to the exercise.

8. When time is up, relax and see how you feel.

9. Practice as often as possible until you can make the switch instantly and feel your anxiety lessen quickly.

Blue Skies, Sitting, Eyes Open

1. Set the timer for 10 minutes.

2. Sit in a chair, feet flat on the floor and hands resting in your lap.

3. Eyes are open.

4. Bring up your feared scene, allowing all the emotions to surface.

5. Begin Yoga Breath and at the same time immediately switch to your Blue Skies image. Connect to all the feelings it engenders.

6. Continue making the change from feared scene to Blue Skies.

7. When time is up, relax and see how you feel.

8. Practice daily.

Blue Skies, Standing

1. Set the timer for 10 minutes

2. Stand tall with your shoulders and head relaxed.

3. Distribute your weight on both legs to feel balanced.

4. Bring up your feared scene, allowing all the emotions to surface.

5. Begin Yoga Breath and at the same time immediately switch to your Blue Skies image and feel your emotions change.

6. Keep switching back and forth until time is up.

7. Relax and see how you feel.

8. Practice daily.

Blue Skies, Walking/Running

1. Set the timer for 10 to 15 minutes.

2. Stand tall with your shoulders and head relaxed.

3. Distribute your weight on both legs to feel balanced.

4. Begin walking and picture your feared scene.

5. Begin Yoga Breath and at the same time switch to Blue Skies.

6. Keep walking and changing from one mental image to the other.

7. Increase your pace to simulate your event, and practice switching under these more demanding conditions. Agility handlers will need to practice going all out in a run.

8. When time is up, relax and see what you've accomplished.

Were you able to make a faster switch on command? Remember, this is another tough technique to master because your feared scene has been with you for a long time, perhaps even for a lifetime. Giving it up is not going to be easy. Handlers who are afflicted with ring nerves often feel tremulous, shaky and unstable. When you're feeling that vulnerable, it's tough to give it your best. The unpredictability of competing can shake you. But with perseverance

Disengaged

Lisa continues, "The worst time is in the waiting area where I can't hide my nerves from my dogs, because when I stiffen up, then they go stiff too and sometimes look away from me. Once I get moving it usually becomes better, but sometimes I have no verbal commands until partway through the course and sometimes not even hand signals, poor dogs! I'm just getting through the course instead of being a good partner to them. If they aren't running well, I feel powerless to do anything. At the end of the run, my mouth is dry and I can't get my breath because I forgot to breathe. In order for me to get through a trial, I have to disappear from the whole thing. I can't be in the ring, be with my dogs. This makes me think about giving up competing, even though I want to go further into understanding training issues, which really does fascinate me."

As Lisa's story demonstrates, it's very easy to get distracted and shaken by dog or handler missteps, especially if you don't feel like you're walking or running on solid ground. Making instant decisions and recovering quickly from mistakes in the ring will be nearly impossible if you have a bad case of ring nerves. But Lisa worked on her training program, practiced all the visualizations and came up with a wonderfully creative safe space, combining aspects from all three.

and practice, you'll acquire the skill to make that immediate mental and emotional switch.

THE BEAM

The *Beam* is an exercise adapted from an acting technique. An actor friend of mine suffered terribly from stage fright. When she became nervous on stage, she felt frightened and unbalanced. She disconnected from her body to block out the audience. In acting class, she learned a technique that kept her feeling firmly planted, helped her become more vocally secure and stable and lessened her anxiety. The actor's nerves are similar to Lisa's experience of disengaging from self, dog and event (see *Disengaged*). The Beam consists of two imaginary rods that run vertically and horizontally through the center of your body, forming an axis in the abdomen. This axis is a mental and physical stabilizer.

Creating the Beam

1. Set the timer for 10 to 15 minutes.

2. Sit in a chair, feet flat on the floor and hands resting in your lap, stand tall and balance your body.

3. Relax your head, neck and shoulders.

4. Close your eyes.

5. Begin Yoga Breath and continue it for this exercise.

6. Imagine a Beam of green light, or any color that you choose. The Beam radiates soothing heat and energy and is stronger than steel. It runs down the center of your body, from the top of your head right into the floor. This is your foundation of support, not rigid or confining, but strong and flexible, allowing you to move with fluidity and confidence.

7. Picture another strong comforting Beam that runs perpendicular to the first one and runs right through your belly button. Try to see and feel the warmth and strength of these Beams: one running from head to floor, the other from belly button to back.

8. These two Beams form a powerful axis at your being's very core, creating a center of power and vitality as well as a place of tranquility. Connecting emotionally with this central point will help you to feel secure, grounded, unshakable and invigorated and able to face the competition's uncertainties.

9. Imagine the Beam. Feel its energy and warmth and see yourself competing as a steady, unflappable handler moving through your event.

10. Continue picturing the Beam until time is up, then relax and see how you feel.

11. Practice daily.

Training Tip

Make the Beam your own. Change the color or have no color; imagine them as solid rods; picture them without heat; let them be anything you want. Whatever you imagine, if you are comfortable with the image and have a strong sense of it, it will work.

Were you able to feel the warmth and energy that radiates from the Beam? Can you clearly picture it? Can you see yourself competing as the successful handler that you want to be? With disciplined practice, the Beam becomes a fundamental part of your person.

The Beam Form

My Beam looks and feels like: _____

_____

_____

_____

_____

_____

My Beam is filled with: _____

_____

_____

_____

_____

My Beam cue word or phrase is: _____

_____

I can use the Beam in the following circumstances: _____

_____

_____

_____

Examples of the Beam

Following are how a few handlers see their Beam:

Handler #1

"I see my Beam as the color of the sun, reddish yellow, and when I close my eyes I imagine its heat running up and down my spine. I feel its energy and power at my core."

Handler #2

"What I've created is blue and cool and soothing at the same time. I see the Beam from my head to the floor as a real stabilizer, making me feel planted instead of out of myself when I get anxious."

Handler #3

"I just couldn't imagine a Beam, so I held an actual metal rod taken from my closet, closed my eyes and pictured two steel rods making the axis. Really touching the rod helped make the image real."

Example of a Beam Form

Following is Lisa's Beam form:

1. **My Beam looks like:** *a wide gold-colored band that is made of rubber or some sort of elastic material and is attached to my shoulder. The other end of this band is attached to my dog's shoulder. It's really a giant umbilical cord that keeps us connected throughout our run, and that grounds me and makes me feel safe. This way I can't disconnect from her when things aren't going well.*

2. **My Beam is filled with:** *telepathic thoughts that run along the band from me to my dog, so she always knows what I want.*

3. **My Beam cue word or phrase is:** *band of gold*

4. **I can use the Beam in the following circumstances:** *during our run, especially when I feel like I'm falling apart and shutting off to cope with ring nerves. It will help me reconnect so I can recover from mistakes quickly.*

The Beam, Standing

1. Set the timer for 10 to 15 minutes

2. Stand tall with your shoulders and head relaxed.

3. Distribute your weight on both legs to feel balanced.

4. Imagine that you're standing at a show, on deck, at the start, etc.

5. Bring up your feared scene, feeling all of the emotions connected to it.

6. Begin Yoga Breath and at the same time see and feel the Beam, how it balances and anchors you. You're solid and secure in your abilities, and your dog can rely on you to be present to experience a great event.

7. Keep switching back and forth, from feared scene to the Beam.

8. When time is up, relax and see how you feel.

9. Practice daily.

The Beam, Walking/Running

1. Set the timer for 10 to 15 minutes.

2. Stand tall with your shoulders and head relaxed.

3. Distribute your weight on both legs to feel balanced.

4. Begin walking and picture your feared scene.

5. Begin Yoga Breath and at the same time switch to the Beam, feeling its radiating warmth and energy. You pull from this core your sureness and vitality. You are unstoppable in reaching the desired goals for you and your dog.

6. Keep walking and changing from feared scene to the Beam.

7. Increase your pace to simulate your event, and practice making a smooth switch from feared scene to the Beam.

8. When time is up, relax and see what you've accomplished.

9. To be able to call on the Beam at a competition, you'll need to practice daily.

THE BUBBLE

The last variation in *Creating a Safe Space* is the *Bubble*, a marvelous mental device that will provide you sanctuary and concealment in the ring. In *That Winning Feeling!* Jane Savoie describes a similar technique she uses to protect herself from negative thoughts. She envisions a transparent bubble around her head and pictures the negative words hitting the bubble and bouncing off. The Bubble keeps her safe from her own negativity as well as other peoples' opinions.

Creating the Bubble

1. Set the timer for 10 to 15 minutes.

2. Sit with feet flat on the floor or stand with your weight evenly distributed.

3. Sit or stand tall. Relax your head, neck and shoulders.

4. Close your eyes.

5. Begin Yoga Breath.

6. Picture yourself and your dog enclosed in a large Bubble that can stretch or contract, giving you total freedom of movement. It keeps you and your dog safely within it, no matter how far away your dog is from you during your event.

7. The Bubble is translucent and makes you invisible to judges, other handlers and spectators. It is lit from within with a warm glow. It creates a comfortable, sheltered atmosphere that no dog show environment can pierce.

8. The Bubble is also filled with high energy, mental toughness, belief in yourself, happiness at being a competitor and anything else you need that will help you reach your goals.

9. Continue breathing and opening to the Bubble.

10. Sit, breathe and etch the Bubble into your mind.

11. Practice daily.

Write down the details of the Bubble.

The Bubble Form

1. **My Bubble looks like:** _____

   _____

   _____

   _____

   _____

   _____

2. **My Bubble is filled with:** _____

   _____

   _____

   _____

   _____

   _____

3. **My Bubble cue word or phrase is:** _____

   _____

4. I can use the Bubble in the following circumstances: _____

_____

_____

_____

_____

_____

Examples of the Bubble

Three handlers describe their Bubble:

Handler #1

"Mine is translucent from the outside in, but transparent from the inside out. I want to see what's happening around me, but when people watch me I get very anxious and can't concentrate. So now, I can be invisible but still see everything that's happening. I filled my bubble with my mother's voice telling me I could accomplish anything I wanted."

Handler #2

"My Bubble is like a cocoon, and when I think of it, I'm safely wrapped in warmth. No one can see me and I can only see my friends who support me. I get calm as soon as I enter it, and so does my dog, because I leave all my fears outside."

Handler #3

"I filled my Bubble with laughter and certain foods that make me feel good when I'm stressed. I'll always feel confident now because the Bubble expands to any size so in Open during the sit stay, when I used to freak out that she'd

A Band of Gold

Lisa's visualizations combined concepts of feeling safe, being grounded and turning off the dog show environment. She practiced cueing herself with "band of gold" to bring up feelings of safety, invisibility and connection. Lisa says, "As I practiced I could see little changes occurring in my usual reactions. I'm shutting down less when I get insecure and staying emotionally with my dog." She continues, "I still have a ways to go to stop ring nerves from hampering our runs, but with my 'band of gold,' and invisible shield, I feel a difference in how I handle my dog. When I make sure I'm breathing, I have lots of energy to spare, and we rock!"

NQ, my dog is still connected and I feel I can communicate with her though I'm out of her sight."

Example of a Bubble Form

Following is Lisa's Bubble form:

1. **My Bubble looks like:** *It's completely transparent, so I'll have a clear view of the course, but it's invisible and I'm invisible when I'm in it. My dog isn't in the Bubble, she's on the course. The Bubble is just for me, to block out peoples' opinions of me.*

2. **My Bubble is filled with:** *confident feelings, my love for my dogs, my love for Agility*

3. **My cue word or phrase is:** *shield*

4. **I can use the Bubble in the following circumstances:** *during our run when my negative thoughts start, and I think people are looking at me and judging my mistakes. Also in training class when sometimes I feel the same way as I do at a trial.*

The Bubble, Standing

1. Set the timer for 10 to 15 minutes

2. Stand tall with your shoulders and head relaxed.

3. Distribute your weight on both legs to feel balanced.

4. Imagine that you're standing at a show, on deck, at the start, etc.

5. Bring up your feared scene, feeling all of the emotions connected to it.

6. Begin Yoga Breath, and at the same time see yourself in the Bubble invisible and protected.

7. Keep switching back and forth, from feared scene to the Bubble. When the time is up, relax and see how you feel.

8. Practice daily.

The Bubble, Walking/Running

1. Set the timer for 10 to 15 minutes.

2. Stand tall with your shoulders and head relaxed.

Training Tip

Use the three visualizations to dominate your feared scene. Imagine details, write it all down, read it out loud, then practice, practice, practice!

Training Tip

Add your dog to your practice sessions for all three visualizations.

3. Distribute your weight on both legs to feel balanced.

4. Begin walking and picture your feared scene.

5. Begin Yoga Breath and at the same time switch to the Bubble, feeling its sheltering quality.

6. Keep walking and changing from feared scene to the Bubble.

7. Increase your pace to simulate your event and practice making a smooth switch from feared scene to the Bubble.

8. When time is up, relax and see what you've accomplished.

9. To be able to call on the Bubble at a competition, you'll need to practice daily.

FURTHER READING

Ken Baum, et al. *The Mental Edge: Maximize Your Sports Potential With the Mind/Body Connection*. Perigee 1999.

Gerald Epstein. *Healing Visualizations: Creating Health Through Imagery*. Bantam Doubleday Dell 1989.

Chungliang Al Huang and Jerry Lynch. *Thinking Body, Dancing Mind*. Bantam Books 1994.

James E. Loehr, Ed.D. *The New Toughness Training for Sports*. A Plume Book 1995.

Jerry Lynch and Chungliang Al Huang. *Working Out, Working Within*. Jeremy P. Tarcher/Putnam 1999.

Robert H. McKim. *Experiences in Visual Thinking* (2nd edition). Brooks Cole 1980.

Steven Ungerleider. *Mental Training for Peak Performance: Top Athletes Reveal the Mind Exercises They Use to Excel*. Rodale Press 1996.

Michael Lee Wright. *800 Stepping Stones to Complete Relaxation: Physical, Emotional, Sleep, Dream, Mental, Creativity, Self, Visualization, Projection*. Wings Publishers 2000.

RESOURCE LIST

Achieve Peak Performance, http://www.peakachievement.com

Better Mental Athletic Performance with Sportslink, http://www. gosportslink.com/en/session.htm

Creating the Life You Want, http://www.innerself.com/Creating_Realities/ Creating_The_Life_You_Want.htm

Harnessing the Power of Visualizations, by Rita Milios, M.S.W., http://www. soulfulliving.com/harnessingthepower.htm

Maximize Sports Performance Through Mental Conditioning, http://www. movementum.com/Mental_cond.htm

Peak Performance, http://performance-media.com/bib.asp

Visualization Technique for Peak Performance, http://www.performance-media. com/visual.asp

Visualize Your Way to Health and a New Life, http://www.mjbovo.com/ Visualizations.htm

Chapter 6

The Confidence Game

You are what you think about all day long.

Dr. Robert Schuller

IN THIS CHAPTER

- Self-Esteem Is a Lifelong Process
- The Origins of Self-Esteem
- Being Aware of Your Self-Image
- Ways to Boost Self-Esteem

> *"The exercise that really threw me for a loop was the Self-Esteem Awareness Questionnaire," says Jane. "I scored below 50! I felt defeated at first, that I'd never be able to pump myself up. But then I reminded myself that I was actually feeling better since I started this program, much less anxious during class and competition, and this would be just something else to fix. I practiced switching from positive to negative, and it was easy to do because I'd been practicing with Blue Skies so the switch was fast from the start, even during class and at the last show I entered. I didn't like doing Angel on My Shoulder alone, my own voice on the tape was too much for me. But one of my best friends trains with me, has ring nerves too, and agreed we could help each other. It's intense to hear my words coming out of her mouth, but I want my negatives to disappear, so I'm sticking with it. I'm still working on making my strengths part of me. For now they feel like a bunch of words, and when I'm nervous it's hard to think of them. But, I keep practicing because I've still got a way to go."*

CONFIDENCE

Throughout this book, we've been talking about how handlers can become confident competitors. All the exercises and techniques you've learned will help you reduce anxiety and achieve success in the ring. However, we have not touched on the major underlying causes of ring nerves: low self-esteem. Chapter One lists some of the causes: heredity, childhood factors, life experiences, etc. Now we'll take a closer look at why many handlers feel insecure and unstable in the ring. Self-defeating attitudes don't spring up out of the blue. They are usually rooted in lifelong beliefs; many are subconscious. Living with the idea that you cannot cope with or take command of life's problems leads to anxiety, feelings of helplessness and low self-confidence. The good news is that we can create a positive self-image of ourselves, which means we can learn to become highly determined and assured beings. To do so takes awareness and hard work. Exercises that bolster self-esteem follow later in the chapter.

Some handlers carry emotional and behavioral baggage that stops them from being the best they can possibly be in their lives. Others are successful personally and professionally, but performing in dog shows triggers fearful reactions that have their origins in earlier unresolved issues. Whatever the reasons for your ring nerves, it is important to look at your self-image.

To reach your potential in your sport as well as in any other challenge, you must have a positive attitude about your capabilities. You must also recognize your shortcomings and work to overcome them.

Many handlers' stories featured in this book serve as demonstrations of the difficulties competitors have. However, even handlers who have titles often

No Confidence

Ellen says, "I began worrying months before a trial fearing that I would embarrass myself at some point. It was just ridiculous, because, though of course I've made mistakes and had disappointments over the years, nothing like I was imagining had ever happened. But I couldn't stop the awful mental pictures I carried around of either my dog running around the ring with everyone laughing because I didn't train her properly, or me completely forgetting the course during Agility and standing in the middle not knowing what to do. I have to admit I resorted to taking tranquilizers to get through shows in the past, and when we did well I never believed that had anything to do with me being a good trainer. I'd also obsess about any mistake for days, even if we had taken home the blue ribbon.

"During the Ring Nerve Seminar I did tell the group about the wall of ribbons I have at home, and most of them couldn't understand why I was there. I just couldn't explain to them that those awards didn't matter, because I could never get my confidence up regardless of how many years of experience I had, or how many titles we won. I took the seminar because I wanted to feel better and see myself as a good trainer who knows what she's doing. When we worked on self-esteem exercises, it really hit me how I belittle myself and that I've never been a confident person."

suffer from low self-esteem since winning may make no difference. They feel they just got lucky and aced their event. These handlers don't connect with their achievements and their confidence level never rises. Every time they compete, they focus on their mistakes, not their triumphs. In one of my ring nerve seminars, a participant who successfully competed in Obedience and Agility for many years shared with the group the admission that she always felt like a loser.

As you read Ellen's story in *No Confidence*, you may recognize parts of yourself in it. The more aware you are about yourself, the more choices you have to make positive changes to your image. Though often a painful process, looking at the reasons for low self-esteem and making those changes will enable you to become the handler you've wanted to be.

Let's look at an important element of confidence: self-esteem.

SELF-ESTEEM

Self-esteem is your own genuine respect and worth. You acknowledge your strengths and limitations, and embrace your own humanness as well as that of others. You believe in your self-worth and go after the things that you want in life. You enjoy a high level of confidence and want to live out your passions. You use your talents for your own well-being as well as giving to the world.

Dog handlers with low self-esteem put themselves down. "I'll never qualify, so what's the use of trying?" they say. They are unable to assert themselves. They won't speak up for themselves. They may think, *I'm uncomfortable with some of my trainer's demands in class, but I'm afraid to talk to him about it because he'll think I'm stupid.*

How could someone have such low self-esteem? Self-esteem is not something you wake up with one day. It is developed over one's lifetime and has its beginnings in childhood. Some possible origins of low self-esteem include:

1. Hereditary Traits

   Anxiety can run in families. If it has affected your family, you may have a propensity for being overly sensitive and may not have learned to cope with these emotions in certain situations. You may feel you have no control over your life.

2. Anxious and Critical Parents

   Self-esteem is a learned behavior. If your parents had a high regard for themselves, were happy and content and allowed for mistakes, then it's likely that you developed into a well-balanced, expressive, confident adult. But if they were anxious, unsatisfied and critical, odds are you developed low self-regard.

3. Loss of Parent

   Divorce, death or separation can lead to chronic feelings of abandonment, anxiety and depression, which impact the development of self-esteem.

Demanding Parents

Ellen says, "I think the reason I've succeeded so well in competitions even though generally I feel anxious and unsure of myself is because I've always had a need to please, which I now recognize as feelings of insecurity. I'm an only child and both my parents were very demanding that I be the best in order to make them happy. If I didn't get straight As, they were both terribly displeased. I knew my mother didn't think she was very capable in life in general. She relied on my father for everything, and she wanted me to be different from her, so she put lots of pressure on me to succeed and lived through my achievements. My father would get angry at me if I wasn't the top student, I think because he worried about how he came across to others as a parent. I hated to let them down. Now, it's terrible for me if I even think about disappointing my dog's trainer by NQing.

"So, no matter what is going on, I've got to be the best, and if I can't get the blue ribbon, I berate myself for being a loser, even though we almost always qualify with high scores. After the Ring Nerve Seminar I continued working on self-esteem and exploring how I really see myself as a person. It was very hard for me to look at things that made me feel so uncomfortable, but once I did, I could figure out how to go about changing. My main goal is being able to feel good about myself, whether I win or lose. The worst truth I had to face was that I never, and I mean never, had fun training or competing with my dogs. That hurt. I used to tell myself it was fun, but with all the anxiety and worry, it was a lie."

4. Addictions

   Adult children of parents who were workaholics, alcoholics, etc. often form low opinions of themselves.

These are only a few of the many reasons that people develop poor self-image. If you see only your limitations and not your strengths or feel incapable of succeeding in or out of the ring, you can still make significant changes over time that will allow you to become a true winner.

Let's return to Ellen's predicament (See *Demanding Parents*). As Ellen worked on her self-esteem, she uncovered how her upbringing influenced the feelings she had about herself as a handler and competitor.

SELF-AWARENESS

It's important to be aware of how you see yourself. With this clarity of vision comes the insight of how you interact and respond to the world around you. This knowledge allows you to set a course of action to make positive changes in your life.

Exercise

1. Write down your answers to the following statements to find out how you feel about yourself as a handler.

2. Take your time and add as many details as possible.

3. Then rate your answers on the Self-Esteem Scale below.

Self-Esteem Awareness Questionnaire

1. I think I'm a good handler within the present limits of my expertise.

   Yes____ No____ Sometimes____

   Why? _____

   _____

   _____

2. I get down and gloomy, and feel overwhelmed at a dog show.

   Yes____ No____ Sometimes____

   Why? _____

   _____

   _____

3. I am easily discouraged and this shows when I am competing.

   Yes____ No____ Sometimes____

   Why? _____

   _____

   _____

4. It is hard for me to ask my instructor or other handlers for help.

   Yes____ No____ Sometimes____

   Why? _____

   _____

   _____

5. I have not entered a dog show because of the way I felt about myself.

   Yes____ No____ Sometimes____

   Why? _____

   _____

   _____

6. I am very critical of myself when I make mistakes.

   Yes___ **No**___ **Sometimes**___

   Why? _____

   _____

   _____

   _____

7. I believe I can accomplish the goals I've set for myself and my dog.

   Yes___ **No**___ **Sometimes**___

   Why? _____

   _____

   _____

   _____

8. It is very important to me that other handlers think I'm a good trainer.

   Yes___ **No**___ **Sometimes**___

   Why? _____

   _____

   _____

   _____

9. I think disparaging and demeaning things about myself in training class and shows.

   Yes___ **No**___ **Sometimes**___

   Why? _____

   _____

   _____

   _____

10. I view my accomplishments as mediocre.

    Yes___ **No**___ **Sometimes**___

    Why? _____

    _____

    _____

    _____

11. When other handlers or my instructor compliment me, I have a hard time believing them.

Yes___ **No**___ **Sometimes**___

Why? _____

_____

_____

_____

12. I am able to speak up for myself at home, work, training class and competitions.

Yes___ **No**___ **Sometimes**___

Why? _____

_____

_____

_____

13. I feel devastated when the instructor in class points out my mistake.

Yes___ **No**___ **Sometimes**___

Why? _____

_____

_____

_____

14. I am envious of other handlers and compare myself negatively to them.

Yes___ **No**___ **Sometimes**___

Why? _____

_____

_____

_____

15. Judges intimidate me.

Yes___ **No**___ **Sometimes**___

Why? _____

_____

_____

_____

16. If my dog NQ's I get very angry at him.

    Yes___ No___ Sometimes___

    Why? _____

    _____

    _____

    _____

17. I take pride in even my smallest achievements in competition.

    Yes___ No___ Sometimes___

    Why? _____

    _____

    _____

    _____

18. I feel I am a good partner to my dog.

    Yes___ No___ Sometimes___

    Why? _____

    _____

    _____

    _____

19. I get excited about taking on new tasks and challenges.

    Yes___ No___ Sometimes___

    Why? _____

    _____

    _____

    _____

20. I enter each show with a positive attitude.

    Yes___ No___ Sometimes___

    Why? _____

    _____

    _____

    _____

21. I feel like an imposter when I do well in the ring.

    Yes___ No___ Sometimes___

    Why? _____

    _____

    _____

    _____

22. I get pleasure from training and competing with my dog.

    Yes___ No___ Sometimes___

    Why? _____

    _____

    _____

    _____

Read over what you've written and rate your answers on the following scale:

Handlers' Self-Esteem Scale

10. _____ Very strong, positive self-image

9. _____

8. _____ High

7. _____

6. _____

5. _____ Middling, needs improvement

4. _____

3. _____

2. _____ Low, you're holding yourself back!

1. _____

A total score of 150–220, indicates high self-esteem; 140–149, you're almost there; 50–100, needs fine-tuning; below 50, roll up your sleeves. No matter what your score, there's always room for improvement. Now let's get to work!

BOOSTING YOUR SELF-ESTEEM

Now that you've read about causes of low self-esteem and taken the Self-Esteem Awareness Questionnaire, it's time to work on changing the negative beliefs you have about yourself into positive ones.

Embracing Positive Self-Talk

Each of us has an internal dialogue running all the time. This dialogue, called self-talk, can be either positive or negative in nature and has enormous emotional significance and repercussions. What we say to ourselves in experiences and situations often decides how we'll feel about them and what action we will take. If you keep saying to yourself, "I always choke and blow the end of our run," it's likely you will.

If your self-image is poor, then the negative thoughts you have probably dominate your self-talk. If so, the success you want for yourself and your dog will be hard to come by. Over time, negative self-talk becomes automatic and habitual and destroys confidence. It's important to remember that you can choose to say positive things to yourself to counter negative self-talk.

Changing Negatives to Positives Exercise

1. Think of three or more negative statements that you say about yourself as a competitor. If none come to mind, read over your Self-Esteem Awareness Questionnaire.

2. Write them down on the form below.

3. Next, write a contrasting positive statement that rebuts your negative one. For example, here's how Ellen countered one of her negative statements:

    Negative Statement: I'm always terrified that I'll lose control of my dog in the ring and look stupid.
    Positive Statement: I'm a very good handler with a well-trained dog, and we both know what we're doing in the ring.
    Now, get going using the following tips for writing positive statements.

Writing Positive Statements

*   Begin all statements with "I" to keep them personal. For example, "I am a great handler."

*   Use positive words in your statements to ease anxiety quickly. For example, do not say, "I'm not going to freak out as soon as I enter the ring," instead, "I do Yoga Breath and calm myself when I enter the ring."

*   Your positive statements have to be forceful and personally meaningful to be able to override the influence of negative statements you may have been carrying around for years.

Negatives to Positives

1. **Negative Statement:** *I*_____

   _____

   Positive Statement: *I*_____

   _____

2. **Negative Statement:** *I*_____

   _____

   Positive Statement: *I*_____

   _____

3. **Negative Statement:** *I*_____

   _____

   Positive Statement: *I*_____

   _____

4. **Negative Statement:** *I*_____

   _____

   Positive Statement: *I*_____

   _____

5. **Negative Statement:** *I*_____

   _____

   Positive Statement: *I*_____

   _____

Now that you've gotten some of your negative thoughts down on paper, we're going to practice switching back and forth between them and their positive counterparts. The goal is to be able to make a mental as well as an emotional switch instantly, even if you're under pressure, as for instance in the show ring.

Switching on Positives/Turning off Negatives Exercise

1. Set the timer for five minutes.
2. Sit in a chair; feet flat on the floor.
3. Have your written statements in front of you.
4. Choose one set of negative/positive statements.

Training Tip

- Write positive statements on 3x5 cards or Post-its and place them throughout your house.

- Start each day off by reading a different positive statement about yourself.

- Keep the written statements in your vehicle at dog shows for a reminder of how wonderful a person and handler you are.

---

5. Close your eyes and think of your negative statement and try to feel all the anxiety you have about it.

6. Begin Yoga Breath and at the same time immediately switch to your positive statement, trying to connect to any feelings it brings up.

7. Continue switching back and forth from negative to positive.

8. When time is up, relax and see how you feel.

9. Practice daily, increasing practice sessions to at least 10 minutes.

10. Practice switching one set of statements at a time.

Did you see any change in your feelings? If not, remember that many of the doubts you have about yourself are cemented in your mind, so chipping away at them will take some time.

Angel on My Shoulder

Angel on My Shoulder is an exercise designed to transform the destructive negative mental talk you play continually into benign noise. By actually hearing these negative words spoken out loud, while being supported by a trusted "angel" and your positive counterstatements, you'll make negative self-talk a thing of the past.

Angel on My Shoulder Exercise

This exercise, one of the most popular in my Ring Nerve Seminars, is powerful in its approach to convert your self-disparaging words into white noise. Listening to your negative statements out loud may sting initially, but with practice they'll become harmless.

Creating Angel on My Shoulder Cards

1. Write three of your self-talk negative statements, one each on a 3x5 card.

2. Write three positive counterstatements, one each on a 3x5 card.

Training Tip

Because of the intense nature of this exercise, begin with one minute and gradually increase to three to five minutes.

Angel on My Shoulder, Solitaire

1. Have a tape recorder with you.

2. Place your three negative statement cards in front of you.

3. Set the timer.

4. In as loud and aggressive a voice as possible, read each of your three negative statements over and over into your recorder until the time is up.

5. Rewind the tape, sit back and relax for a few minutes.

6. Now place your three positive statement cards in front of you.

7. Gently touch your left shoulder with your right or left hand. This soft contact is important for making the connection to your positive self.

8. Turn on the recorder loud, and as you listen to your negative statements, at the same time, in a low calm voice, keep repeating your positive statements, until the tape stops.

9. Sit back, relax and think about what happened, and then on the page below write down your experience.

Record how you felt during *Angel on My Shoulder*. What was your reaction as you listened to your own negative words? Were you sad, angry or shocked? Did you laugh or cry? Did any or all of the positive statements dominate after a while? Did some of the negative ones hang on tight or become white noise? If they did, how did that make you feel?

Angel on My Shoulder Experience

1. **This exercise made me feel** _____

_____

_____

_____

_____

_____

2. **My negative statements** _____

_____

_____

_____

_____

_____

3. **My positive statements** _____

_____

_____

_____

_____

_____

4. **Other comments** _____

_____

_____

_____

_____

_____

Angel on My Shoulder for Two

1. Find another handler, family member or friend whom you trust and feel comfortable with.
2. Give your negative statement cards to your partner.
3. Hold your positive cards, and with your right or left hand, gently touch your left shoulder.
4. Stand very close to each other, face to face.
5. Set the timer.
6. When time begins, have your partner read aloud your negative statements over and over, in an aggressive voice.
7. At the same time, whisper the positive counterstatements to yourself.

8. When time is up, relax and write down your experience on the lines below.

9. If your partner wants to change his or her negative self-talk, switch places.

10. Practice at least three times a week, increasing time to five minutes.

Angel on My Shoulder Experience

1. This exercise made me feel _____

_____

_____

_____

_____

_____

2. My negative statements _____

_____

_____

_____

_____

_____

3. My positive statements _____

_____

_____

_____

_____

_____

4. Other comments _____

_____

_____

_____

_____

_____

Angel on My Shoulder for a Small Group

1. Gather together three to five handlers, family members or friends whom you trust and feel comfortable with.

2. Have each person prepare their negative and positive statements on 3x5 cards.

3. Choose which handler will go first, and have that person hold their positive cards.

4. Choose the "angel" who will place their right hand gently on the handler's left shoulder.

5. Choose two "devils" who will hold the handler's negative statements, and have them stand very close to the handler, face to face.

6. When time starts, the devils read the handler's negative statements repeatedly in loud aggressive voices.

7. At the same time, the angel continually whispers into the handler's left ear the positive counterstatements.

8. When time is up, relax, talk about how you feel and write it all down on the *Angel on My Shoulder Experience* pages.

9. Have each group member take turns as the "handler."

10. Try to get together at least once a week to practice.

Angel on My Shoulder

Ellen first experienced *Angel on My Shoulder* in a group at my seminar. "I was frightened to do this in front of people because I am so embarrassed about the way I feel. But as each handler took a turn, it was such a relief to hear how they felt about themselves, and that I wasn't alone. In fact, one woman in my group began to cry when she heard what she had been saying to herself for years. That helped a lot, because I, too, felt like crying during my turn. *Angel on My Shoulder* had a huge effect on me that day. It made me determined to stop hurting myself with these terrible thoughts.

"I decided to continue *Angel on My Shoulder* in the solitaire version, I don't know or trust anyone close to have as a partner. The first time I played that recording of negative statements, I was shocked. I heard my own voice come back at me with the same tone that my father used when he got angry. It was hard to keep listening. When I first started I only listened to half the tape, but I kept increasing the time and also practiced switching from negative thoughts to positive ones. Diane was right, it takes a while, a long while sometimes, but I began to feel better. Slowly I came to believe the positive things about myself. The last time I competed in Obedience, I went into it with a more positive attitude and actually had some fun."

Fill in with *Angel on My Shoulder, Solitaire* to turn off negative self-talk and turn on those positive expressions!

Angel on My Shoulder Experience

1. This exercise made me feel _____

   _____

   _____

   _____

   _____

   _____

2. My negative statements _____

   _____

   _____

   _____

   _____

   _____

3. My positive statements _____

   _____

   _____

   _____

   _____

   _____

4. Other comments _____

   _____

   _____

   _____

   _____

   _____

Recognize Your Strengths

Realizing what your strengths are will be difficult if you're constantly putting yourself down. The following exercise asks you accept that you are a capable, accomplished, talented, loving, wonderful person and handler. You'll write down these truths about yourself. The second part has you think why it may be difficult to accept your accomplishments. Use the following tips to guide you.

Tips for Seeing Strengths

1. Be very detailed and specific in your responses in order to make them meaningful.

2. Use "I" statements to make these words, ideas, statements part of you.

3. Write anything that comes to mind; get a stream of consciousness going.

4. The big successes or achievements are wonderful, but don't forget that all the small stuff adds up to big stuff!

My strengths are: _____

_____

_____

_____

_____

Finding my strengths was hard because: _____

_____

_____

_____

_____

Seeing Strengths Example

Ellen wrote down her strengths:

My strengths are: *I'm kind because I'm very willing to help other handlers, in or outside of class, who are struggling in either Obedience or Agility. I'm a smart dog trainer and understand animal behavior and know how to get my dogs to respond in the way I want. I'm very patient, and know that training my dogs to do well takes time. I'm loving because I have good relationships with my husband, children, dogs and friends.*

Finding my strengths was hard because: *It was hard to think about some of these things, but even harder to write them down and then to read it over because I felt like such a show-off. I was taught that bragging about oneself is not nice. Writing about my strengths just feels strange. I'll have to keep practicing.*

PRACTICING SELF-ESTEEM EXERCISES

Add the Self-Esteem Exercises to your daily training program so you will appreciate yourself as an extraordinary person and dog handler. Be aware of your behavior and look for the meaning behind it. When you find yourself with negative thoughts, switch to positive thoughts. Don't attribute your successes, big or small, to luck; instead, celebrate your effort and ability. Positive attitude is everything if you want to get on the road to success!

FURTHER READING

Elaine N. Aron. *The Highly Sensitive Person: How to Thrive When the World Overwhelms You*. Broadway Books, 1997.

Dale Carnegie. *How to Develop Self-Confidence and Influence People* (reissue). Pocket Books, 1999.

Melanie Fennell. *Overcoming Low Self-Esteem*. New York University Press, 2001.

Alanna Jones. *104 Activities That Build: Self-Esteem, Teamwork, Communication, Anger Management, Self-discovery, and Coping Skills*. Rec Room Publishing, 1998.

Phillip McGraw. *Self Matters: Creating Your Life from the Inside Out*. Free Press, 2003.

Matthew McKay and Patrick Fanning. *Self-Esteem: A Proven Program of Cognitive Techniques for Assessing, Improving and Maintaining Your Self-Esteem*. New Harbinger, 2001.

Glenn R.Schiraldi, Ph.D., et al. *The Self-Esteem Workbook*. New Harbinger, 2001.

RESOURCE LIST

National Association for Self-Esteem, http://www.self-esteem-nase.org

Building Self-Esteem, http://www.more-selfesteem.com

Self-Esteem, http://www.selfesteemworld.com

Self Esteem Learning Foundation Homepage, http://www.selfesteemshop.com

Self-Confidence: UIUC Counseling Center, http://www.couns.uiuc.edu/Brochures/self.htm

Mind Tools: Sports Psychology and Self-Confidence, http://www.mindtools.com/selfconf.html

Building Self-Esteem and Self-Confidence, http://www.counsel.ufl.edu/selfHelp/selfEsteem.asp

Chapter 7

You'll Make Mistakes!

The greatest mistake you can make in life is to be continually fearing you will make one.

Elbert Hubbard

IN THIS CHAPTER

- What Is Perfectionism?

- The Characteristics of Perfectionists

- How to Turn off Perfectionist Self-Talk

- Why Should I Plan to Make Mistakes?

> *"I was okay with the exercises until it came to making mistakes in class and at events," says Jane. "I know how low my self-esteem is and I've struggled to stop the 'shoulds' and 'musts' my whole adult life, so there were no surprises for me. But I never thought I would be able to intentionally set out to make mistakes. It helped me to look at my fears in a specific way, because I think of myself as being terrified of everything having to do with competition, but when I had to write down specific statements, I saw that some things didn't bother me as much. For example, I'm not as afraid to make a mistake in front of the judge as I thought I'd be. But how other handlers view me, whether in class or at a competition, is a bigger deal for me. Making the list helped me to see that some fears didn't have the same effect on my nerves. So making a mistake in front of the judge became my number one, easiest feared mistake.*
>
> *"For months I visualized making my mistake in front of the judge in fantasy, trying to make it feel as real as possible. I experimented switching off anxiety with Blue Skies, one of my favorite techniques, until I could cut the tension in just a few seconds. I even practiced this visualization standing so I could go right to Focusing on My Feet to stop the negative mental chatter."*

PERFECTIONISM

A perfectionist lives a philosophy that requires meeting highly unrealistic goals. The perfectionist couples this with a belief that self-worth is determined strictly through accomplishment. Perfectionists don't allow for their own or anybody else's humanness. They can't accept that we all live in a flawed world. Their rigid thinking is loaded with words like "must" and "should." They spend their lives striving to reach the unattainable and in the process must fail.

Handlers who operate under the weight of perfectionism experience the following:

- Increase in their tension and anxiety

- Fear of taking risks in training class and the ring

- Never knowing the personal fulfillment of a job well done

- Depriving themselves of enjoyment

- Generally achieve much less success

When you're expecting a flawless performance from yourself and your dog every time you enter the ring, you're setting yourself up for failure and disappointment. Perfectionism is an internal learned coping mechanism. The good news is that it can be unlearned. As we have seen before, the beginning of change is awareness.

CHARACTERISTICS OF PERFECTIONISTS

- Fear of making mistakes

- Fear of failure

- Unrealistic expectations of self and others

- Disappointment and critical attitude if outcome is not faultless

- Too much concern with minor mistakes

- Chronic worry that the wrong thing was said or done

- Ignoring accomplishments

- Fear of disapproval

- Black-and-white thinking

- Belief that others easily achieve success

- Low self-worth

- Frequent use of the words "should," "must," "have to"

Can't Make Mistakes

Lenny discovered Agility when he retired as a corporate executive four years ago. "My wife competed in Obedience for years, but I never got involved because I didn't have the time. When family friends had to relinquish their Border Collie, Mia, I took her. Mia had finished Basic Obedience and was beginning Agility classes. I continued with her in class and really liked it.

"I've always been a stickler for details, so no matter what I'm engaged in it has to be perfect. I like to have total control over everything I do. Until Agility and ring nerves, I'd never stopped to look at myself. I was a workaholic and never took the time to do any kind of self-examination. But Agility has floored me, I think because now I have to rely on a partner, and a canine one at that. I know Mia is sensitive to everything I feel, but I can't get my nerves under control. I never realized how being a perfectionist can create so much anxiety, though I've always been very tense and have had family members tell me how rigid my thinking was.

"What's driving me crazy is how obsessed I am about making any kind of mistake, even in class. I tell myself to stop thinking this way, it's ridiculous, but I can't stop it. It's gotten so bad that I've been having trouble concentrating, and have forgotten the course more than once. I felt humiliated. A few weeks ago my wife told me she didn't think I was having any fun, and that I was making it tough for Mia too. She's right. I've been using Yoga Breath and the other exercises, but I've got to break through this obsession about not making mistakes."

- High level of anxiety
- Negative comparison of themselves to others
- Difficulty in forming close, honest relationships
- Use of words such as "every," "always," "never"
- Chronic burnout and fatigue

ARE YOU A PERFECTIONIST?

Being aware of your behavior is necessary to end the pursuit of unrealistic, unachievable goals. As you learn how your reactions and responses to others and life situations block you, you'll be able to make the changes necessary to free yourself from perfectionism.

Perfectionist Self-Talk

Following are a list of words and phrases that perfectionist handlers often think and use.

Exercise I

Do you say any of the following about yourself? Check all that apply and add some of your own. Next, go back and counter each negative word or phrase with positive, affirming words and phrases.

For example: N̶X̶ I'm stupid. *P I'm intelligent.*

N=negative word or phrase; P=your positive word or phrase.

N__ I always trip P_____

N__ I'm clumsy P_____

N__ I'm ugly P_____

N__ I'm a failure P_____

N__ I'm lazy P_____

N__ I'm weak P_____

N__ I'm fat P_____

N__ I'm overly sensitive P_____

N__ I'm inadequate P_____

N__ I'm selfish P_____

N__ I have no talent P_____

N__ I'm foolish P_____

N__ I'm bad P_____

N__ I'm wrong P_____

N__ I always screw-up P_____

N__ I'm an idiot P_____

N__ I'm too critical P_____

N__ I'm stubborn P_____

Add some of your own:

N_____   P_____

N_____   P_____

N_____   P_____

N_____   P_____

N_____   P_____

Exercise II

Read over the words and phrases you have checked or written down. Become conscious of the negative, perfectionist self-talk you use throughout the day. Change to your positive words and statements. Awareness of your thinking is the key here. As you slowly change what you think and say about yourself, your thought patterns will alter. You'll begin to internalize and carry the affirming messages into every area of your life.

Exercise III—Turning off Negatives/Switching on Positives

1. Set the timer for five minutes.

2. Sit in a chair, feet flat on the floor and hands resting in your lap.

3. Have your written words and phrases in front of you.

4. Choose one set of negative/positive words or phrases to work on.

5. Now, close your eyes and think of this negative word or phrase and try to feel all the anxiety you have about it. Continue for about 30 seconds.

6. Begin Yoga Breath, then immediately switch to your positive word or phrase, trying to connect to any feelings it brings up.

7. Continue switching back and forth from negative to positive.

8. When time is up, relax and see how you feel.

9. Practice daily, increasing sessions to at least 10 minutes.

10. Practice the switch one set of negative/positive words or phrases at a time.

Did you see any change in your feelings? If not, remember many of the rigid perfectionist words or phrases you think and say to yourself began in childhood, so changing them will take some time.

Perfectionist Awareness Statements

The following exercise will help you to neutralize the rigidity of perfectionist thinking and see the reality of the circumstances and situations you find yourself in.

Training Tip

Practice the switch from negative perfectionist thinking to positive validating thoughts every time you train your dog alone or in class.

How to Fill out the Perfectionist Awareness Exercise

1. In the "negative" spaces below list five perfectionist statements you say about yourself as a competitive handler.

2. Write a realistic counterstatement in the "positive" spaces.

3. Take your time and add as many details as possible to your answers.

Perfectionist Awareness Exercise

Write your perfectionist statements and then write a practical positive response to counter each one.

1. **Negative Statement:** _____

   _____

   _____

   Positive Statement: _____

   _____

   _____

2. **Negative Statement:** _____

   _____

   _____

   Positive Statement: _____

   _____

   _____

3. **Negative Statement:** _____

   _____

   _____

   Positive Statement: _____

   _____

   _____

4. **Negative Statement:** _____

   _____

   _____

Positive Statement: _____

_____

_____

5. Negative Statement: _____

_____

_____

Positive Statement: _____

_____

_____

Example of Perfectionist Awareness Exercise

Here are Lenny's examples:

1. **Negative Statement:** *After competing for over a year, I feel like I should never make any mistakes. When I do, I feel like a failure.*

    Positive Statement: *That's irrational. Everyone makes mistakes, and it's okay. I can learn from the ones I make, to become a better handler over time.*

2. **Negative Statement:** *I'm always afraid at the start that I'll forget the course, look like a fool and the other handlers will think I don't know what I'm doing.*

    Positive Statement: *I have forgotten the course and nothing terrible happened—it's just part of learning. I don't know what other handlers are thinking; most likely it's not about me.*

3. **Negative Statement:** *We must qualify with high scores at the next show or my instructor will think I'm not serious about competing in Agility.*

    Positive Statement: *We will try to qualify with high scores, but if we don't I'm still a successful handler who is getting better all the time. We train and practice hard and my instructor knows how important Agility is to me.*

Turning off Negatives/Switching on Positives

In this exercise, practice switching from negative statements to positive ones, so that your positive side will dominate even if you're under intense show pressure.

1. Set the timer for five minutes.

2. Sit in a chair feet, flat on the floor and hands resting in your lap.

3. Have your written statements in front of you.

4. Choose one set of negative/positive statements.

5. Close your eyes for 30 seconds and try to feel the anxiety you have about your negative statement.

6. Begin Yoga Breath and at the same time switch to your positive statement, trying to connect to any feelings it brings up.

7. Continue switching back and forth from negative to positive.

8. When time is up, relax and see how you feel.

9. Practice daily, increasing sessions to at least 10 minutes.

10. Practice the switch, one set of negative/positive statements at a time.

Did you see any change in your feelings? If not, keep in mind that many of the perfectionist statements you say about yourself you've been saying for years. Have patience—change will come!

MAKE MISTAKES TO FREE YOURSELF!

Think about what it feels like when you fail. Picture yourself in the obedience ring, and your dog messes up on a heeling pattern or picks up the dumbbell and brings it to the judge instead of to you. In agility, you forget the course, while your dog improvises and sets her own course. Do these images get your heart racing and send your anxiety through the roof? Are you thinking, "I'd die if that happened to me?" Most of us respond with some level of discomfort when we blow it, fail, are rejected or fall flat on our faces. But sooner or later we learn the lesson and move ahead. Someone with perfectionist thinking, however, will go into a tailspin and take another hit to their already low self-esteem. They don't learn from the experience, and they begin the cycle again when the next mistake occurs.

Being frightened of making mistakes is a major barrier to success as a competitive handler. In this next section, you'll be asked to deliberately make mistakes in order to learn that they no longer have any power over you. Mistakes are just part of being human and are vital in helping us to learn, grow and move toward our goals. We can't help making mistakes, but we can help how it affects us.

Think about young children just learning to walk or talk. They try to walk, fall, get up and try again. In order to learn to walk they must risk falling. To learn to communicate they must mispronounce or misuse words.

That's what you did as a child so that someday you could read, write and run. You had to begin someplace and you made tons of mistakes to get where you are now. Think about other things in your life you've struggled to master: calculus, playing a musical instrument, driving a car, using a computer, training your dog or learning to compete. Somewhere along the line, perfectionism became ingrained, but you have a chance to change that now.

By consciously making mistakes and learning how to cope with them, you will be facing your fears and feelings about not being perfect and will allow yourself to be human. You'll also become more relaxed and able to set realistic, achievable goals and your confidence and self-image will improve. You'll see how much more successful you can be and how much fun you can have as a competitor.

Planning to Make Mistakes

Complete the following exercise, then practice visualizing yourself making mistakes while being relaxed. The next step, really making errors during training and competition and coping with how that feels, is a great way to take command of perfectionism. Doing so will markedly decrease ring nerve symptoms.

Writing It Down

1. Reread your Perfectionist Awareness Assessment and choose three to five mistakes you are afraid to make. These are your *feared mistakes*.

2. List them from least anxiety producing to most, and write them down in the spaces below.

For example, here is one of Lenny's feared mistakes:

Feared Mistake #1: I'm afraid I'm going to forget the course and look stupid. Now write down your mistakes:

Feared Mistake # 1: I'm afraid _____

_____

Feared Mistake # 2: I'm afraid _____

_____

Feared Mistake # 3: I'm afraid _____

_____

Feared Mistake # 4: I'm afraid _____

_____

Feared Mistake # 5: I'm afraid _____

_____

Visualizing Mistakes

1. Set the timer for five minutes

2. Sit in a comfortable chair, feet flat on the floor and hands cradled in your lap; or lie down, hands resting at your sides, legs relaxed and slightly apart.

Training Tip

Work on one feared mistake at a time and only begin with another when you have actually made the mistake, have faced doing so and your anxiety has eased.

3. Relax your head, neck and shoulders.

4. Bring up the image of your feared mistake, and all the anxiety you have about it.

5. At the same time, begin Yoga Breath and let your body go slack.

6. See yourself making your feared mistake, keep looking at it and let the anxiety surface.

7. While you relax your entire body, think about allowing yourself to make this mistake.

8. Keep relaxing into the image of your feared mistake.

9. Practice daily until your anxiety about making this mistake has lessened considerably.

Making Mistakes

Now you're going to plan to make your feared mistake during a training class and then at a competition. Planning to do what frightens and causes anxiety is the best way to take command of fears. Before you begin, make sure you are well practiced in the exercises and techniques from Chapters 2 through 5, such as Yoga Breath (Chapter 2) and Go With the Flow loosening techniques (Chapter 4).

Planning Your Mistakes

In the spaces below, plan which mistake you are going to make, where and when you are going to make it and what techniques you are going to use to help yourself to cope.

Feared Mistake #1: _____

_____

I plan to: _____

_____

Techniques I plan to use: _____

Where: _____ When: _____

What happened?: _____

_____

_____

_____

_____

_____

_____

_____

Feared Mistake #2: _____

_____

I plan to: _____

_____

Techniques I plan to use: _____

Where: _____ When: _____

What happened?: _____

_____

_____

_____

_____

_____

_____

_____

Feared Mistake #3: _____

_____

I plan to: _____

_____

Techniques I plan to use: _____

Where: _____ When: _____

What happened?: _____

_____

_____

_____

_____

_____

_____

Planning Your Mistakes, Example

Lenny's examples follow:

Feared Mistake #1: *I'm always afraid I'm going to forget the course, look stupid and we'll bomb.*

I plan to: *deliberately not pay attention when I walk the course.*

Techniques I plan to use: *Yoga Breath before and during class, Go With the Flow loosening while making the mistake, Focus on My Body to stop negative thoughts*

Where: *training class* **When:** *this coming Tuesday and again on Saturday*

What happened?: *This was one of the hardest things I've done in a long time. I didn't tell anyone in class what I intended to do, so that increased my anxiety. To purposely not pay attention made my head ache—talk about being uncomfortable! But I did it. And I didn't know where to send my dog in the course. I did this throughout the class, and since they're so used to me trying to be perfect, they knew something was up. I was trying to let it all go and not make a big deal of it. I was even able to*

Letting Go

"As hard as it is to let go of being a perfectionist, I'm determined to do it," Lenny says. "I've practiced on four of my feared mistakes in training class for a month, and I see that the obsession to reach some crazy 'ideal' that can never be reached can destroy my life. I'm slowly getting used to being okay with mistakes, and I am less tense and anxious about them in class. My next goal is to intentionally make these mistakes at a real show. That's going to be very hard to do, but I plan to forget the course at a show coming up next month. My wife thought I was nuts when I started doing this, but she's seen the difference in me, and is beginning to use these techniques to help her with her own ring nerves in Obedience."

tell another handler that I was just having an off day! I used all the techniques I planned on, but my anxiety stayed pretty high. This is going to take a lot of practice.

HANDLING PERFECTIONISM

Perfectionism kills success and stops you from living a happy, rich full life. It creates a cycle of fear, disappointment, low self-worth, depression and chronic anxiety. The exercises in this chapter can be intimidating, especially "Planning to Make Mistakes," but give them a try and add them to your training program. Being free from perfectionist thinking and behavior is worth the hard work and struggle. If you're working this program, I know you have the determination and courage to do it.

FURTHER READING

Martin M. Anthony and Richard P. Swinson. *When Perfect Isn't Good Enough: Strategies for Coping With Perfectionism.* New Harbinger, 1998.

Cynthia Curnan. *The Care and Feeding of Perfectionists.* North Star Publications, 1999.

Jan Goldberg and Caroline Price. *Perfectionism: What's Bad About Being Too Good* (revised). Free Spirit Publishing, 1999.

Thomas S. Greenspan. *Freeing Our Families from Perfectionism.* Free Spirit Publishing, 2001.

Enid Howarth and Jan Tras (contributor). *The Joy of Imperfection.* Fairview Press, 1996.

Allan E. Mallinger and Jeannette Dewyze. *Too Perfect: When Being in Control Gets Out of Control* (reprint). Fawcett Books, 1993.

Ann W. Smith. *Overcoming Perfectionism: The Key to Balanced Recovery.* Health Communications, 1990.

RESOURCE LIST

Perfectionism, http://www.nexus.edu.au/teachstud/gat/peters.htm

Perfectionism, http://www.potsdam.edu/COUN/brochures/perfectionism.html

Perfectionism Tool for Personal Growth, http://www.coping.org/growth/perfect.htm

BBC-Science Human Body-Mind-Perfectionism, http://www.bbc.co.uk/science/humanbody/mind/surveys/perfectionism/index.shtml

Perfectionism, http://www.dundee.ac.uk/counselling/leaflets/perfect.htm

What is Perfectionism?, http://www.utexas.edu/student/cmhc/booklets/perfection/perfect.html

Chapter 8

Goals: A Road Map to Success

A dream is just a dream. A goal is a dream with a plan and a deadline.

Harvey Mackay

IN THIS CHAPTER

- Dreams Beg for Fulfillment

- Finding Your Purpose

- Setting Your Goals

- Breaking Down Big Goals

- Reaching Your Goals

> *"I love these exercises!" Jane says. "Breaking down big goals into small pieces made me feel better almost immediately. Before just thinking about getting a title and having to cope with ring nerves seemed as overwhelming as me trying to get to the moon. Also I think making myself sit down and write out a plan of action instead of just keeping my dreams in my head and not believing I could ever reach them really gave me the feeling of having quite a bit of control. I wrote out two lists of goals to achieve, one for training class and the other for competition. It helped me to practice each of my goals in the safety of class first. Then I could experiment using the exercises from the program to see what was successful for me, and write down what worked and what didn't for each situation. Every morning I read through the goals I'm working on and I believe that is keeping me focused."*

DREAMS

This chapter shows how the goal-setting process influences your ability to conquer ring nerves. We begin with *dreams*, move on to *finding your purpose, goal setting, breaking large goals into small manageable pieces* and, finally, *reaching your goals*.

"*I want to compete in Obedience.*"

"*I want to be a great dance partner in Freestyle.*"

"*I want our CD, our CDX, UDX, OTCH, MACH, MAD, U-ACH, NATCH.*"

"*I want us to compete at Excellent and Master Levels; I want to become an Obedience instructor.*"

"*I want us to win Best in Show.*"

"*I want to be a great competitive team in a number of different sports.*"

"*I want to become a judge.*"

Maybe these were the dreams you had when you became interested in being a competitive dog handler. Maybe you were on the way until ring nerves waylaid you and you quit. Possibly you never got into the ring because you were too afraid to risk it. Perhaps you're still plugging away, but thinking about that title overwhelms you. Maybe one ring nerve experience after another has flattened your self-esteem and now you don't believe you can accomplish what you thought you could. Perhaps your dreams are vague: "I want to win titles some day." Possibly you haven't dared to dream big because you're a nervous wreck.

Whether your dreams are clear and specific or indefinite and hazy or whether they are modest or grandiose, they are important in this ring nerve training program. They are the beginning steps toward your empowerment and success.

Having a dream is great, but it's not enough to get you what you want. Many people never realize their dreams and relegate them to lifelong fantasies. They watch others live their dreams in real life. Some people sabotage themselves along the way. However, to turn dreams into tangible results, you must set goals. Listed below are some reasons why people squelch their dreams:

1. Fear of failure

2. Fear of success

3. Low self-esteem

4. Fear of change

5. Concern about what others might think or say

Too Shy to Compete

Nancy adopted Molly, a mixed breed who was relinquished to a local shelter because of various behavioral problems. "I do some volunteer work for the shelter and had taken Molly for walks. She was a very frightened dog and barked and lunged at other dogs and even people when she was nervous, but when she felt safe she was loving and sweet. So, of course, home she came.

"I've had dogs all my life but never really trained one. Now faced with Molly's reactions I had to get help for both of us. I found a good trainer and Molly showed how smart she was immediately, she really took to the training and so did I. I loved it and found myself wanting to work with Molly all the time. I began to think about competing with her in Obedience and Agility.

"We continued getting increasingly better and my instructor asked me to sign up for her competitive classes. But I've always been very shy and nervous and even though I badly wanted to compete, I couldn't imagine myself stepping into the ring without panicking. Actually, my dream is to compete and become a professional instructor. I talked to my family and a close friend about competing and having a career as a dog trainer, and they all said pretty much the same thing: I was too shy to get up in front of people. I have no confidence and I knew I was holding myself back. So I signed up for Diane's Ring Nerve Program, and little by little it's helping me gain confidence."

6. Fear of the unknown

7. Not wanting to feel uncomfortable

8. Apprehension about the responsibility of getting what they want

9. Not knowing how to set up a plan of action to achieve goals

10. Feeling overwhelmed and guilty about living fully

What are your dreams? What stops you from realizing them?

As Nancy explains in *Too Shy to Compete*, her fears held her back and people who were close to her reinforced them. Follow your own path, no matter how hard that might be. After three months in the Ring Nerve Program, Nancy entered a Match Show.

"I was very nervous, but my goal was just to enter and have us practice competing, and that's what we did, and that felt great!" Nancy says. "On the way home from the show I thought that my dreams aren't so crazy after all, and I'm going to try to reach them all someday."

EXAMPLES OF HANDLERS' BIG DREAMS

- **Handler # 1:** "I want to become a professional dog handler."

- **Handler # 2:** "I want to get both an OTCH and MACH on all of my dogs."

- **Handler # 3:** "I want to write a book about training rescued dogs to become champions."

WHAT ARE MY DREAMS? WHAT HINDERS ME?

1. In the pages below, write down the dreams you had for yourself and your dog when you first began competition training. If you had none, write down what you dream about now.

2. Before you write, sit for a few minutes doing Yoga Breath to relax yourself and unlock your mind to the infinite possibilities. Then be truthful about the stumbling blocks you put in your own way.

3. Dream big! Be specific. Be detailed. Write as if you're painting a picture of your dreams.

4. Face your fears and inhibitions about getting what you want. Detail these as well.

5. When you're finished, relax for a few minutes and read what you've written.

6. Repeat this exercise from time to time to uncover new ideas to pursue, and to stay aware of self-sabotaging behavior.

   Use the following questions as a guide to get your creative juices flowing:

- What kind of a dog trainer do I want to be?

- What kind of a competitor do I want to be?

- What titles do I want to win? How many times?

- What dog sports do I want to excel in?

- How many dogs do I want to train and compete with?

- What shows/arenas do I want to compete in?

- Besides competing, what else in the dog world do I want to achieve? Instructor? Judge?

My dreams for myself as a handler are: _____

_____

_____

_____

_____

_____

_____

My dreams for my dog(s) are: _____

_____

_____

_____

_____

_____

_____

I stand in my own way because: _____

_____

_____

_____

_____

_____

_____

FINDING YOUR PURPOSE AS A HANDLER

The Random House Dictionary defines the word *purpose* as "1. the reason for which something exists or is done. 2. an intended or desired result; end; aim; goal. 3. determination; resoluteness." When you have purpose, you exhibit tenacity, drive and a stick-to-itiveness that will help you break down your ring nerve barriers. You'll make sacrifices, remain motivated, face the unknown and never give up trying. Determining your purpose as a competitive handler is your first step toward goal setting. It is bigger than your goals for it characterizes what your life as a handler is all about. Your goals evolve out of your values. Think of your purpose as your mission statement. When the going gets tough in or out of the ring or when stretching yourself as a handler elicits fear and anxiety, your purpose or goal is the driving force. Your purpose statement is a framework for the decisions you will make and the actions you will take. It will determine who you want to be as a handler and what goals you want to realize.

In the exercise below, compose your purpose statement using the following guidelines:

- Keep it simple, brief and to the point
- Let it flow naturally from your values and passions.
- Use "I" statements to make it personal.
- Write it from your heart, and let it excite and inspire.

Use the following value-laden words to exemplify what you believe in. Add any others that come to mind:

__ skillful

__ smart

__ creative

__ efficient

__ dynamic

__ honest

__ fair

__ loyal

__ courageous

__ friendly

__ realistic

__ competitive

__ energetic

__ strong

__ empathic

__ determined

__ insightful

__ likeable

__ cooperative

__ sensitive

__ funny

__ open

__ organized

__ quiet

__ introspective

__ loving

__ other _____

Exercise

1. Sit in a comfortable chair and begin Yoga Breath to relax and open your mind. Read the words you have checked.

2. Begin writing down what comes to mind on the Worksheet below. Don't force it; take your time.

3. When your purpose statement shines, write it down in My Purpose Statement.

Worksheet

_____

_____

_____

_____

_____

_____

My Purpose Statement

_____

_____

_____

Blind Luck

Barbara had a Collie whom she took to Basic Obedience classes. She loved the training and decided to become a competitive handler. At her first show, she became nervous and could barely finish her event. Barbara continued training her dog, hoping to become a better handler in time. She wanted to win titles, but her nerves got in her way. Her instructor recommended that Barbara add some mental training to the dog training, but she continued in the same way, thinking things would change when she had more experience. Her inability to qualify frustrated her and her ring nerves worsened with each competition. It continued this way until Barbara rescued a blind Collie named Brucie.

"That Collie made all the difference. I am a retired teacher for the blind, and knew what people could overcome to lead full rich lives. When I saw Brucie listed on a rescue site, I had to have him. I knew I could train him and set a goal to compete with him in Rally-O. I wanted to show people that 'disabled' does not mean 'not able.' That's when I attended the Ring Nerve Seminar and began working on myself as well as Brucie's training. It's hard to retrain myself, to change my thoughts and how I behave when I'm feeling stressed, things I've done my whole life, but I wanted to be the best partner to Brucie so he could blossom and be his best, too. Brucie is a love, very smart and has his CGC. He also became a therapy dog and works with children who are physically ill or disabled. Kids love him; after all, he's one of them. Oh, he's doing very well in Rally-O too, we both are. He motivates me every day to grow as a person and a handler, and inspires everyone he touches."

Barbara's story is a perfect example of finding purpose as a dog handler. Her statement reads, "I am determined to become a strong trainer so both Brucie and I reach our potential. I also want to use my skills to demonstrate to others that being blind is not a barrier to achievement, and that rescues have a lot to offer."

SETTING GOALS

We spend much of our lives setting and trying to reach goals. Our goals can be trivial, such as "I've got to make liver brownies for Fido tonight," or they can be important: "By the end of next year I want us to have our UD." In this section, we're going to use goal setting to help you define and achieve your aims, to keep you on track, to stop you from setting yourself up to fail, to boost your confidence and to reduce the symptoms of ring nerves.

Write down your objectives. Having them in front of you makes them real and achievable. Detailed goals written very specifically are a map for the road to success. This roadmap works whether you are just a beginner or are a seasoned veteran. Breaking down larger goals into smaller ones is a way to set yourself up for success every time you step into a training class or competition ring.

Small Goals Equal Big Victories

A goal is a problem you must solve. You decide you want a certain outcome and now you have to figure out how to get it. For example, you want your dog to get his CD later this year but you have ring nerves. You enter shows, but you're not qualifying. You're feeling frustrated and down about not progressing. Your nerves intensify with each show you enter. That CD looks more out of reach than ever. Even thinking about it overwhelms you.

There is an answer: *partialization*. Partialization is a technique for breaking down large goals into the smallest possible pieces and then working on each piece one small step at a time.

Partialization Benefits

Partialization will:

- Reduce feelings of being overwhelmed

- Lessen tension and anxiety

- Allow you to take immediate action

- Stop you from setting yourself up to fail

- Boost your confidence quickly

- Keep you motivated

- Let you take command of the problem

- Keep you on track with its details

- Markedly reduce ring nerves

Guidelines for Setting Goals

1. Write down your goals and keep them handy to read, revise and keep you focused. Working on your goals daily will help internalize them and make them real and reachable.

2. List long-term and short-term goals.

3. Add a timetable to each goal. For example, "I'll have Brucie competing in Ralley-O by April 2004." Even if you need to adjust the timeframe, deadlines keep you focused.

4. Use "I" statements to keep them personal.

5. Goals should be specific and measurable so you can evaluate your progress easily and revise if necessary.

Step by Step

Paula was a handler who wanted her CD within a year. Her friend's dog obtained her CD in her first year of competition, so Paula was determined to do the same. She and her dog are at a level in training where they are ready to compete. But she has ring nerves. As soon as Paula steps into the ring she starts trembling and she seems so freaked out during the exercise that it looks like she's never taken one training lesson in her life.

"When I see the judge standing there I just panic. I'm very aware that people are staring at me, watching me self-destruct, and that bothers me too." Paula's dog is acutely aware that something is wrong with her and regularly tries to leave the ring during their event. They hadn't qualified once since they began competing and things were just getting worse. "I had it in my mind that I must get that CD in a year's time or else, but when I think back on it I was completely overwhelmed."

Paula attended a Ring Nerve Seminar. "I'm so thankful for the breathing exercises; they've helped a lot. I continued working with Diane and we set up a training program with reasonable goals that I could meet on a daily, weekly and monthly basis. My larger end-of-year goal was of course that CD. I broke down getting that CD into the tiniest pieces I could because I needed to lift my self-confidence, fast. I also didn't enter any shows for about three months until I felt I had the breathing and other exercises down pat. It worked! After the first week that I achieved the goals I set out for myself, I knew I would get that CD some day, and finally, after months of practice, we got our first leg.

"What I love about the written goal plan is that when my anxiety starts and I mess up in the ring, I can revise my goals and make the next step even smaller, so that I can succeed the next time around. I don't ever want to go back to feeling so badly about myself. I like staying in control of me."

6. Make goals challenging but able to be achieved quickly for a fast start, and to build your confidence.

7. Rank goals from easiest to most difficult.

8. Break down larger goals into the small manageable steps you need to take.

9. Describe how ring nerves are holding you back.

Use the pages below to write down your top three goals.

My Goal Pages

Goal # 1: _____

_____

My ring nerves keep me from reaching my goals in the following ways:

1. _____

_____

2. _____

_____

3. _____

_____

4. _____

_____

5. _____

_____

These are the small steps I need to take to reach my goal:

1. _____

_____

2. _____

_____

3. _____

_____

4. _____

_____

5. _____

_____

These are the results I would like to see in:

1. 1 week _____

_____

2. 1 month _____

_____

3. 3 months _____

_____

4. 6 months _____

_____

5. 1 year _____

_____

_____

Additional notes: _____

_____

_____

Goal # 2: _____

_____

My ring nerves keep me from reaching my goals in the following ways:

1. _____

_____

2. _____

_____

3. _____

_____

4. _____

_____

5. _____

_____

These are the small steps I need to take to reach my goal:

1. _____

_____

2. _____

_____

3. _____

_____

4. _____

_____

5. _____

_____

These are the results I would like to see in:

1. 1 week _____

_____

2. 1 month _____

_____

3. 3 months _____

_____

4. 6 months _____

_____

5. 1 year _____

_____

Additional notes: _____

_____

_____

Goal # 3: _____

_____

My ring nerves keep me from reaching my goals in the following ways:

1. _____

_____

2. _____

_____

3. _____

_____

4. _____

_____

5. _____

_____

These are the small steps I need to take to reach my goal:

1. _____

_____

2. _____

_____

3. _____

_____

4. _____

_____

5. _____

_____

These are the results I would like to see in:

1. 1 week _____

_____

2. 1 month _____

_____

3. 3 months _____

_____

4. 6 months _____

_____

5. 1 year _____

_____

Additional notes: _____

_____

_____

To add more goals either copy the My Goals pages or write them in your Ring Nerve Journal.

Example of a Goal Page

Here is one of Nancy's Goal Pages:

Goal # 1: CD

My ring nerves keep me from reaching my goals in the following ways:

1. *I have no confidence in my abilities.*

2. *Preshow anxiety builds for weeks before show.*

3. *On day of show I'm irritable, nauseous and very tense.*

4. *On deck I get light-headed and shaky; sometimes I feel like I have to go to bathroom.*

5. *As soon as I enter the ring, my body trembles and I feel frightened, have no ability to concentrate and can't breathe.*

These are the small steps I need to take to reach my goal:

1. *Stop entering shows for a while.*

2. *Use Yoga Breath and other exercises throughout the day and in training class.*

3. *Work on not comparing myself to others.*

4. *Set up some private lessons with my instructor in addition to classes before I begin competing again.*

5. *Make having fun with my dog a major goal of competition.*

These are the results I would like to see in:

1. 1 week: *I want to learn how to breathe to relax in and out of the ring.*

2. 1 month: *I want to be using all the exercises without thinking about how to do them.*

3. 3 months: *I want to begin entering match shows, especially to compete in places where I had had a meltdown and felt embarrassed.*

4. 6 months: *Enter trials to get leg for CD.*

5. 1 year: *I want to have the CD or be very close to it, with scores in the high 190s. Want to feel confident even when we make mistakes, and have fun though we don't do well.*

   Additional notes: CD *within 18 months*

Visualizing Your Goals

To help you internalize and realize each of your goals, practice visualizing yourself having achieved them. Try the following exercise.

1. Set the timer for five minutes.

2. Sit in a chair, feet flat on the floor and hands resting in your lap; or lie down, hands resting at your side, legs and feet relaxed and slightly apart.

3. Choose one large or one small goal to picture.

4. Begin Yoga Breath.

5. Close your eyes and visualize yourself having achieved this goal. See all the details of accomplishing it, and feel all the emotions that this will evoke.

6. Continue seeing and feeling all the positive results of your achievement.

7. When time is up, relax and see how you feel.

8. Practice daily, increasing practice sessions to at least 10 minutes.

9. After you reach one goal, choose another and repeat this exercise.

Did you feel what it would be like to reach your goals? What were the feelings that came up with this image of success?

Your Road to Success

The road you take won't be a smooth one. You must expect and accept detours, potholes and a bumpy ride. You may even encounter a washout along the way. Keep in mind that progress is always two steps forward and one back, but each time you fall back, it's not as far as the last time. It is important that you believe that as long as you keep trying, you'll always move ahead.

STEP BY STEP

Don't put off setting down your goals. Don't let big dreams overwhelm you. Break it all down into little pieces, work on each piece one step at a time and before you know it, your anxiety will lessen and your confidence will rise. Start today!

FURTHER READING

Sean Covey. *The 7 Habits of Highly Effective People*. Simon & Shuster, 1998.

Jeff Davidson. *The Complete Idiot's Guide to Reaching Your Goals*. Alpha Books, 1997.

Anna Juarez. *The Setting Goals and Achieving Them Method*. Anna Juarez, 2002.

Talane Miedaner. *Coach Yourself to Success: 101 Tips from a Personal Coach for Reaching Your Goals at Work and in Life*. McGraw-Hill Contemporary Books, 2000.

Brian Tracy. *Goals! How to Get Everything You Want—Faster Than You Ever Thought Possible*. Berrett-Koehler Pub., 2003.

Zig Ziglar. *Goals: How to Set Them, How to Reach Them*. Nightingale-Conant Corporation, 1989.

RESOURCE LIST

Goal Setting: Making and Keeping Goals, http://www.goal-setting-and-keeping-personal-goals.com

Goal Setting: The Secrets to Reaching Your Full Potential, http://www.runwithsam.com/mot_goal_setting.html

Reaching Your Goal, http://www.decision-maker.net/goals.html

Goal Setting Inspirational Quotes, http://www.topachievement.com

Goals and Goal Setting, http://www.mygoals.com

Personal Goal Setting, http://www.time-management-guide.com

Personal Goal Setting: Mind Tools, http://www.mindtools.com/page6.html

Chapter 9

Competing From Your Core

I am centered and nothing can disturb the calm peace of my being.
Anonymous

IN THIS CHAPTER

- What Is Core?

- Connecting to Core

- Centering and Core

- Moving Smoothly in the Ring

"I've been working on the Ring Nerve Program for quite a while now, learning how to relax, face my fears, increase my self-esteem, trying to drop being perfect and concentrate, no matter what is happening around me," says Jane. "For me, the Core has brought all the elements of the program together. I see it as a binder for everything I've learned; it ties one thing to the other. When I practice the exercises and techniques, I always do it now with an image of my core. It took daily practice to really get the feeling of what center is, and I do move easier when I'm connected to it. Sometimes an exercise helped me find it. For example, when I breathed, I took it right through my 'physical core' and down into my feet, and focused on them. Once I was into 'the here and now,' then everything flowed because I wasn't worrying about anything. Or I've used my image of 'core' to help me feel grounded.

"The last time I felt panicky was two matches ago. I was able to visualize the drawing of 'Core' that I had made, and it helped me to stay with Go With the Flow exercises to face my fears. I've really begun to see a change in myself and in Goldie as far as our ring nerve symptoms are concerned. The biggie is that I'm not as afraid anymore. It takes a while to see that change, I think, because fear was such a part of my life in the ring. It felt weird at first. I noticed it at an Obedience trial I entered that in the past would have freaked

141

me out. I was able to keep myself from the 'what ifs' and never got super anxious. I had what I would describe as intense butterflies, which I could handle, and we qualified with a score of 180.

"Diane says that mental training never stops, it just changes over time, and I agree. I've gone from putting all my effort into stopping ring nerves so I can get back into competition, to including some work on enhancing the mental aspect of my performance. I've written a weekly personal program for practicing that includes looking at my goals, noting any changes and making revisions to them. I've still got a way to go to conquer my ring nerves, but I feel I have great tools to use to get where I want to go."

THE CORE

Ring nerve symptoms create a disordered mental state making it almost impossible to focus or concentrate in competition. Since performance anxiety is a mind/body condition, the effects on our physical state will be just as severe. It makes us feel shaky, uncoordinated and clumsy and throws all the dog's training off. Moving well with him in the ring becomes an impossible feat. The solution can be found in learning about and competing from a place within the mind and the body called the Core.

The Core is a mental and physical source of power. The mental component of Core is your own energy. The center lies a few inches below your belly button. The Core is equivalent to chi or ki, the basic flow of life energy in Eastern culture. Learning to make a mental connection to this force will help conquer ring nerves. The Core's physical aspect controls breath, movement and stability. It centers itself in the abdominal muscles and muscles within the torso and pelvic area.

Each aspect of Core has a major influence on the other. In this chapter, we'll work on developing both the mental as well as the physical Core, which will help stop ring nerve symptoms and enhance competitive performance.

Characteristics of Competing From Your Core:

- Emotional centering
- Reduced anxiety and tension
- Good posture
- Competing in the here and now
- Accepting and coping well with emotions
- Physical balance
- Simultaneously tranquil and alert
- Feeling grounded

- Ability to move smoothly

- Lowered risk of muscle strain

- Ability to focus intently

- Being open and aware

- Ability to accept and deal with difficult circumstances

In the sections below, you'll work on exercises to help you connect with your Core. This will enable you to choose to feel balanced and centered. It will counteract being agitated and awkward in the ring.

Before connecting to Core.

After connecting to Core.

CREATING AN IMAGE OF YOUR MENTAL CORE

Making your Core into a visible entity with form, shape and color, will help you summon it when competition anxiety has you feeling off-balance. In the pages below, describe your Core in detail and then draw it. Writing a description and then picturing it will help make it tangible. Reread "Characteristics of Competing From Your Core" to guide you. Note: Drawing skills are not necessary for this exercise!

Exercise I: Visualizing the Core

1. Have pencil, pen, colored pencils, crayons, etc., on hand.

2. Set the timer for three to four minutes.

3. Close your eyes.

4. Sit in a chair. Begin Yoga Breath and relax your whole body.

5. Exhale and inhale deeply through your nose. Visualize your breath reaching your Core. Feel it touch your Core.

6. To help you focus on the Core, gently touch that spot with your fingers, a few inches below your belly button.

7. Sit deep into your Core. Feel yourself connect with it. Feel how centered and balanced you are in the chair.

8. Imagine what this central powerhouse looks like. Physically it contains muscles, tendons, arteries and capillaries, a spine that allows your body to move and bend and be balanced among its many other functions.

9. Keep picturing this important place. Does it have shape? If so, what shape is it? Is it colored? Clear? Translucent? Does it have depth? Is it flat? Is it bright? Does it shine? Is it dark? Dim? Does it move? Vibrate? Is it still? Is it hot? Cold? Smooth or rough? What emotions does it contain? Fear? Anger? Enjoyment? Love and passion? What does your Core consist of? Vitality? Force? Strength? Stamina? Verve?

10. Form an image of your Core, and when you have it, describe it in the space below. Be as detailed as possible.

Exercise II: Written Description of Core

My Core is: _____

_____

_____

_____

_____

_____

_____

_____

_____

_____

Now, draw your Core in the space below.

Exercise III: Visual Image of Core

My Core Looks and Feels Like:

Exercise IV: Connecting With Your Core

1. Reread your Core description and look at your Core drawing.

2. Set the timer for two to three minutes.

3. Sit tall, feet flat on the floor, hands resting in your lap; or lie down, arms resting at your sides, legs relaxed and slightly apart.

4. Relax your head, neck and shoulders.

5. Close your eyes and bring to mind the image of your Core.

6. Begin Yoga Breath and relax into your Core. Feel each long, smooth, deep breath go to the very essence of your being.

7. Keep those images in mind and at the same time feel your breath as it touches your Core, the seat of your strength and energy as well as a source of tranquility and serenity.

8. Feel the connection with your Core. Feel how balanced your physical and mental nature is.

Finding Her Center

Beth attended a Ring Nerve Seminar because she had lifelong performance anxiety; nevertheless, she wanted very much to compete in Obedience. "I've always accepted that I couldn't do many things because of my anxiety, but when I discovered Obedience, I decided it was time to change things. I want to be a competitive handler very much, or at least try to be one. My dog is a very young English Setter, so we're learning together, but my anxiety spikes even in training class and I'm afraid I'm ruining him before he has a chance to begin showing.

"It seems as if I've always suffered from nerves. Sometimes my neck and shoulders ache for days after I leave class. From childhood on, I'd been told I was clumsy, but I never made the connection that this had something to do with my nerves. And it's a big problem for me in Obedience because I'm often tripping over my own feet while heeling and on turns. I always feel off balance. When I watch myself practice in class in front of the mirrors, I'm embarrassed at what I look like. My body is stiff as a board and my shoulders are up around my ears. I'm so unsteady from nerves, I feel like I'm going to keel right over. Jesse is young and pretty frisky, but when I get very nervous he gets totally out of control. My instructor has tried to help me calm down, but I can't. When I read that the Ring Nerve Seminar would emphasize feeling grounded and walking smoothly, I signed up immediately.

"I've worked hard practicing Yoga Breath and focusing, and that has helped, but learning about the Core and using the breath and visualizations to get myself centered has really made a difference. I've been practicing from the Core for months and several times reached a point where everything in class just came together. When that happened, Jesse was much calmer and really paid attention. During one of those moments, while we practiced a heeling pattern, he was looking at me strangely like he never had before. It was funny, but he almost seemed confused. I don't think he's used to me being calm and centered even for a moment.

"It's been very hard retraining myself and I know I have a long way to go. But with every small change comes the belief that I'm getting somewhere, and I know that Jesse and I will compete some day."

9. Continue linking the vitality of Core to your mind and body.

10. When time is up, relax and reflect on how you feel.

11. Practice visualizing your Core throughout the day.

Were you able to feel your Core? Were you able to imagine what it looks like? Did you feel centered? Daily practice will be required to stay connected to your Core when you're experiencing ring nerves and are off-center during a competition.

Adding Core-Centering Statements

As we have seen, positive statements are potent tools in conquering ring nerves. Use the following examples of affirming statements to add to your Core exercises. Compose your own and write them on the pages below.

Positive Statements for Core-Centering

- "I am centered and strong and can reduce ring nerve anxiety even during my event."

- "Breathing through to my Core keeps me mentally and physically balanced during competition."

- "I accept the ups and downs of competition."

- "When my dog makes a mistake, I can stay grounded for both of us."

- "I stay open to the competition experience."

Exercise V: Writing Positive Core Statements

Core Statement #1: _____

_____

Core Statement #2: _____

_____

Core Statement #3: _____

_____

Core Statement #4: _____

_____

Core Statement #5: _____

Exercise VI: Repeating Core Statements

1. Set the timer for two minutes.

2. Sit in a chair feet, flat on the floor and hands resting in your lap; or lie down, legs and feet relaxed and slightly apart.

3. Begin Yoga Breath and relax your entire body.

4. Breathe deeply, slowly and smoothly into your Core.

5. Then, breathing normally, slowly repeat one of your affirming statements out loud until time is up.

6. Try to connect with the feelings of the statement.

7. When time is up, relax.

8. Practice this exercise daily, increasing time to five minutes.

Work on one or more affirming Core statements at a time. Daily practice is necessary to make these statements a powerful force to counter ring nerve symptoms.

THE PHYSICAL CORE

The physical ability to walk, run, bend and turn smoothly and to control posture and balance is a function of the abdominal region. In physical and sports training it's called the Core. It's the body's nucleus of power, found in the lower trunk musculature.

Major Muscles of the Abdominal Core

1. **Rectus Abdominis**: flexes the trunk

2. **External Obliques**: flexes and laterally bends the trunk

3. **Internal Obliques**: flexes and laterally bends the trunk

4. **Transversus Abdominis** (deep abdominal muscle): compresses the abdomen

5. **Erector Spinae** (lower back muscle): extends spine.

Core Conditioning

Conditioning, strengthening and toning your physical Core through regular exercise will have a major effect on ring nerves. Being fit means being confident. If you feel strong in your body, it will affect your ability to concentrate under pressure and manage performance anxiety. This book is not about physical fitness, but knowing a little about and being aware of the physical aspect of your Core is important when you're trying to stay connected to its mental counterpart. Below is an easy Core warm-up. The exercises that follow teach you to work from your Core. In the Further Reading and Resource List sections at the end of this chapter, you will find information about fitness and Core conditioning.

Exercise I

1. Sit tall in a chair, feet flat on the floor and hands resting in your lap.

2. Gently pull your belly button back toward your spine, hold and breathe easily for 10 seconds. If you can, slowly pull your belly button back a little further and hold for 10 seconds.

3. Concentrate on breathing easily into your Core.

4. Relax for 10 seconds and then repeat exercise 10 times.

5. Practice daily.

Exercise II

1. Sit tall in a chair, feet flat on the floor and hands on the arms of the chair.

2. Pull your belly button back toward your spine and at the same time push your elbows gently down on the armrests. Breathe and hold the position for 10 seconds.

3. Your shoulders will come down and your shoulder blades will come together slightly.

4. Relax for 10 seconds, then repeat exercise 10 more times.

5. Practice daily.

WORKING FROM YOUR CORE

The following exercises are tune-ups for connecting with your Core in various positions that you will find yourself at a show. Practice daily in every training session to prepare yourself to *compete from your Core*.

Sitting

1. Set the timer for five minutes.

2. Sit in a chair feet, flat on the floor and hands resting in your lap.

3. Begin Yoga Breath and watch each breath. Go deep into your Core.

4. At each exhale, gently pull your belly button back toward your spine and feel your shoulders come down. Make sure you are sitting tall with your shoulders relaxed.

5. At the same time you breathe into it, bring up the mental picture of your Core.

6. Sit deep in your chair, breathing into your Core, seeing its image.

7. Verbalize your statements to help you connect.

8. When time is up, relax and see how you feel.

9. Practice daily.

Standing

1. Stand tall and balance your weight on both legs to help center yourself.

2. Begin Yoga Breath and watch each breath. Go deep into your center.

3. At each exhale, gently pull your belly button back toward your spine and feel your shoulders come down. Make sure you are standing tall with your shoulders relaxed.

4. In your mind's-eye, see the image of your Core.

> **Training Tip**
>
> Practice the Core Warm-ups at shows to connect both physically and mentally with the Core.

5. Continue standing, breathing and connecting to your Core. Feel how grounded and stable you are.

6. Repeat your statements to help you connect.

7. When time is up, relax and see how you feel.

8. Practice connecting with Core throughout the day.

Walking/Running

1. Stand tall and balance your weight on both legs.

2. Begin Yoga Breath and watch each breath. Go deep into your center.

3. At each exhale, gently pull your belly button back toward your spine and feel your shoulders come down. Make sure you are standing tall with your shoulders relaxed.

4. See the image of your Core in your mind.

5. Repeat your statements to help you connect.

6. Begin to walk slowly, keeping the breath smooth, your belly button gently pulled back toward your spine, your shoulders down and relaxed.

7. Keep walking and concentrating.

8. Pick up the pace to a fast walk, trying to stay focused on your Core.

9. If you're in Agility, practice at a run.

10. Keep practicing until time is up.

11. Relax and see how you feel.

12. Practice connecting throughout the day.

How to Practice at Home, Work and Play

Make a conscious effort to connect with your Core throughout the day, so in competitions you can tune into it in a moment in various situations:

1. Sitting at the kitchen table

2. Standing in the shower

3. Walking to your vehicle

4. Sitting in your vehicle, standing outside of it, walking to a destination

5. Walking in the supermarket, standing on line

6. Walking in your house

7. Sitting at your desk/computer

8. Sitting in a movie theater

9. Sitting at a sports event

10. Running to catch a plane

11. Running through the park

12. Walking/running with your dog

Practicing Connecting With the Core for Competitions

1. Before you get out of bed in the morning

2. In the house getting ready to leave

3. Standing while you put collar/harness/leash on your dog

4. Walking your dog to vehicle

5. Sitting in your vehicle on the way to class or show

6. Sitting in vehicle at show before you get out

7. Walking/trotting into class/show site

8. Sitting at show waiting for event to begin

9. Walking/running with your dog to the potty area

10. Walking/trotting/running in the ring

11. Waiting in the on deck position

12. Standing at the start

13. Entering the ring

14. Standing, walking/running in the ring

Training Tip

Practice connecting to Core at least three times a day.

Not connected to your Core.

Competing from your Core.

Sitting: Turning on Core and Facing Your Feared Scene

1. Go back to Chapter 4 and review visualizing your feared scene, trying to evoke the anxiety you feel when you experience it.

2. Review "Creating an Image of Your Mental Core."

3. Set the timer for five minutes.

4. Sit in a chair feet, flat on the floor and hands resting in your lap.

5. Bring up your feared scene and the anxiety you have about it.

6. Keeping your feared scene up, switch into your Core, visualizing what it looks like, feels like and what you wrote about it. Feel yourself in this fantastic state of centeredness and balance, open to anything and ready to take on the competitive dog world, even in the face of your feared scene.

7. Use your Core Affirming Statements to help you move into your center.

8. Continue being balanced.

9. When time is up, relax and see how you feel.

Were you able to be centered when you pictured your feared scene? Getting to your Core and staying there is difficult, especially during competition.

Standing: Turning on Core and Facing Your Feared Scene

1. Set the timer for five minutes.

2. Stand with your head, neck and shoulders relaxed.

3. Bring up your feared scene and the anxiety you have about it.

4. Keeping your feared scene up, begin Yoga Breath and breathe right into your Core.

5. Use your Core Affirming Statements to help you move into center.

6. Concentrate on continuing to stay centered.

7. Continue standing and breathing down deeply into your Core.

8. When time is up, relax and see how you feel.

How did it feel facing your feared scene? Did being centered make it easier to face? Connecting with Core and staying there is difficult, especially during competition, but with practice you'll be able to do it.

Walking/Running: Turning on Core and Facing Your Feared Scene

1. Set the timer for 10 minutes.

2. Stand tall with head, neck and shoulders relaxed.

3. Bring up your feared scene and the anxiety you have about it.

4. Begin Yoga Breath.

5. Start walking slowly.

6. Use your Core Affirming Statements to help you move into center.

7. Be sure to keep your shoulders back and relaxed.

8. Continue walking and pick up the pace while staying connected to Core.

9. Practice in a run if necessary.

10. When time is up, relax and see how you feel.

Did changing your pace trip you up? Could you stay connected? With time and practice, you will.

Putting Core Exercises Together

Note: The following exercise requires a full-length mirror.

1. Set the timer for 10 to 15 minutes.

2. Sit in a chair feet, flat on the floor and hands resting in your lap.

3. Begin Yoga Breath, and watch each breath. Go deep into your Core.

4. At each exhale, gently pull your belly button back toward your spine and feel your shoulders come down.

5. As you breathe into your Core, bring up its image.

6. Sit deep in your chair; continue breathing into your Core.

7. Stand up, trying not to break the connection. Feel its power to ground and center you.

8. Remain standing and breathing for about 10 seconds.

9. Next, bring up your feared scene, feeling all the anxiety it evokes.

10. Start walking, breathing into your Core, feeling centered while thinking of your feared scene.

11. Walk slowly back and forth in front of a full-length mirror. See how balanced you look, what strength of presence you have, the vibes of confidence you radiate.

12. Increase your pace to simulate your event, staying connected to Core, while facing your fears in the competitive ring.

13. Practice daily and these positive feelings and good posture will become natural.

14. Practice in your training facility first without, and then with, your dog.

Recording Your Core Experiences

As your training program develops, record your Core experiences in both training and competition. You will be able to make changes and note your progress. Reread the introduction to this chapter, the characteristics of Core and your Positive Core Statements to guide you. Either photocopy the section below, or continue it in your Ring Nerve Journal.

My Core Experiences

I am working from my Core when: _____

_____

_____

_____

_____

Date: _____ Where: _____

I am working from my Core when: _____

_____

_____

_____

_____

Date: _____ Where: _____

I am working from my Core when: _____

_____

_____

_____

_____

Date: _____ Where: _____

FURTHER READING

Derek Brigham. *Bullet-Proof Abs: 2nd Edition of Beyond Crunches*. Dragon Door Publications, 2000.

Gerg Brittenham. *Stronger Abs and Back: 165 Exercises to Build Your Center of Power*. Human Kinetics Pub., 1997.

Colleen Craig. *Abs on the Ball: A Pilates Approach to Building Superb Abdominals*. Inner Traditions Intl. Ltd., 2003.

Daniel Goleman. *Emotional Intelligence* (reprint). Bantam Books, 1997.

Richard Strozzi Heckler, ed. *Being Human at Work: Bringing Somatic Intelligence into Your Personal Life*. North Atlantic Books, 2003.

Richard Strozzi Heckler. *Holding the Center: Sanctuary in a Time of Confusion*. Frog Ltd., 1997.

RESOURCE LIST

The Emotions and Centering, http://www.lovesedona.com/07.htm

The Importance of Grounding and Centering, http://www.shakticenter.com/grounding.html

Pilates, the Core and the Evolution of Mind-Body, http://www.byregion.net/articles-healers/pilates.html

Strengthening Your Core, http://www.hughston.com/hha/a_15_2_3.htm

Strengthening and Toning: Core Training, http://www.ivillage.co.uk/dietandfitness/getfit/strengtone/articles/0,9544,269_171310,00.html

Chapter 10

Stretching: Loosen and Energize

If at sixty you are supple and strong, then you are young.
Joseph Pilates

IN THIS CHAPTER

- Why You Should Stretch

- How to Begin Stretching

- Easy to Do Stretches

> *"I have to admit I haven't done any regular exercise for years,"
> says Jane. "I walk and exercise my dogs—that's it. So I wasn't
> thrilled to add stretching to my program, but Diane insisted I give
> it a try. I did, and I'm enjoying it. I do at least the walking in place
> warm-up and full-body stretch before every class. I add more
> stretches before competing, and always do the neck rolls and shoul-
> der shrugs, while I'm waiting in the on-deck position. I also pulled
> out my Richard Simmons video a month ago and I work out with
> that two times a week. I'm thinking of trying a six-week beginner
> Yoga class because I'd like to learn how to meditate. I believe that
> will really help me beat ring nerves!"*

STRETCHING

One manifestation of ring nerves is severe body tension. It signals your dog that
in this particular show, competing is not a good thing and maybe even scary.
Your dog then considers it something to be avoided. A body that is loose and
supple will not only help you to move in the ring, but will help you conquer
ring nerves. In this chapter, you'll learn simple stretching exercises that you
can use at home, training class and competitions. The exercises offered in this
chapter are just a sampling. The Further Reading and Resource List at the

chapter's end give more resources. Stretching is one of the first things you should practice before going into the ring.

A daily regimen of stretching tones your body and calms your nerves. Stretch before and after every training class and competition to loosen your muscles and energize your body. Regular stretching offers many rewards. It is an important part of your ring nerve training program.

The Benefits of Stretching

- Reduces muscle tension

- Relaxes entire body

- Allows for freer movement

- Increases range of motion

- Prevents injuries, such as muscle strain

- Promotes circulation

- Increases strength and stamina

- Increases focus and concentration

- Decreases stress

- Improves sleep

- Improves posture

- Improves balance

- Helps loosen the mind's control of the body

- Promotes an overall sense of well-being

- Feels good!

When you're feeling very anxious, stretching is a quick way to alleviate anxiety by working out body stiffness and tension.

A Quick Stretch

Try this simple exercise while you're reading this book.

1. Sit tall, shoulders relaxed, feet flat on the floor.

2. Breathe naturally.

3. Look up toward the ceiling and at the same time stretch both arms up over your head, reach for the ceiling, stretch as far as you can comfortably. Do not strain.

Feeling Good

4. Hold for 10 seconds. Slowly bring arms down, rest your hands in your lap.

5. Repeat two more times.

Didn't that feel good? Imagine how you'll feel after you've stretched out your whole body! Now, let's get to the stretches.

Rules and Guidelines for Stretching

- Check with your physician.

   Before you do the stretches, have a physician examine you for any medical conditions.

- Does a stretch look too difficult? Move on!

  Don't do any stretches that you think will be too strenuous. Choose others.

- Warm up before stretching.

  To lessen the chance of muscle strain, warm up for five to ten minutes before you begin your stretching routine. Include Yoga Breath too, for overall relaxation.

- Stretch before every training session or competition.

  Stretching gradually increases heart rate, gets your blood flowing and increases body temperature. Muscles become supple and flexible and the body readies itself for activity that is more strenuous.

- Stretch after every activity.

  Cool down for relaxation, to prevent sore muscles, improve flexibility and gently return body to a resting state.

- Do not bounce while in a stretch.

  Holding the stretch will lengthen muscles. Bouncing can cause injuries and pain.

- Do not strain or force the movement.

  You should feel no pain or discomfort after you've stretched. If you do, then you've overextended the stretch.

- Do not hold your breath.

  Keep breathing slowly and smoothly to keep yourself relaxed and help focus on the stretch.

- Increase the hold gradually.

  Stretch to the point where you feel slight tension and initially hold stretches for five to ten seconds. Gradually work up to between 15 to 20 seconds. The object is to get the feeling of tension to slowly subside as you hold the stretch.

- When you move into a stretch:

  Exhale through your mouth.

Training Tip

Do not get discouraged if you feel awkward at first and find some stretches difficult to do. With practice they will become easier and you'll see great results in how you feel and move.

- When you move back to the start position:

  Inhale through your nose.

- Keep your back straight.

  Concentrate on keeping your lower back straight but relaxed during these exercises.

  Focus on stretching.

  Concentrate on the muscle being stretched and every movement during the exercise.

- No pain:

  Stop immediately if you feel pain during an exercise. If pain persists, see your physician.

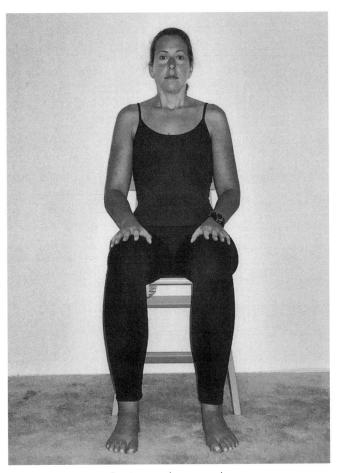

Getting ready to stretch.

- Sets:

  Work up to two or three sets of repetitions for each exercise. Don't rush it; take your time and go at your own pace.

- Practice days:

  Stretch at least three times per week.

Stretching Exercises

The simple stretches that follow offer rewards of mental and physical well-being when included in a multidimensional training program. Be sure to read the guidelines carefully before you begin.

Warm-Up I

1. Stand with feet together.
2. Breathe naturally.
3. Bring arms up as if you were going to run.
4. Begin walking in place.
5. Increase pace slowly.
6. Decrease the pace for the last 60 to 90 seconds.
7. Continue for five to ten minutes.

Warm-Up II

1. Take your dog for a walk for five to ten minutes.
2. Begin slowly and gradually increase to a moderate pace.
3. Decrease the pace for last 60 to 90 seconds.

Warm-Up Breath

1. Sit comfortably in a chair, feet flat on the floor.
2. Breathe slowly in through your nose, keeping your breath deep and smooth, then exhale slowly and smoothly through your mouth.
3. Repeat two more times.

Neck Rolls

1. Sit comfortably in a chair, feet flat on the floor, hands resting in your lap.
2. Slowly bring your chin to your chest and feel your neck elongate.

Training Tip

Before you begin each stretch, make sure you have the correct form.

3. Hold this position for a few seconds while breathing in through your nose and out through your mouth.

4. Slowly roll your head toward your left shoulder.

5. Bring your left ear down toward your left shoulder and hold for five to ten seconds. Do not strain.

6. Continue breathing in through your nose and out through your mouth.

7. Slowly roll your head toward your right shoulder.

8. Bring your right ear down toward your right shoulder and hold for five to ten seconds. Do not strain.

9. Breathe in through your nose and out through your mouth.

10. Slowly roll your chin back to your chest and hold for a few seconds.

11. Bring your head up and relax.

12. Repeat two more times each side.

Shoulder Shrugs

1. Sit comfortably in a chair, feet flat on the floor, hands resting in your lap.

2. Take a deep breath in through your nose, and slowly raise your shoulders toward your ears.

3. Hold for at least five seconds.

4. Exhale through your mouth and push your shoulders down toward the floor.

5. Hold for at least five seconds.

6. Inhale and raise your shoulders toward your ears.

7. Hold for five seconds.

8. Exhale and push your shoulders down toward the floor.

9. Hold for at least five seconds.

10. Relax, let your hands rest in your lap and breathe easily.

11. Repeat two more times.

Stretch your neck.

Roll to the left.

And now to the right.

Arm and Shoulder Stretch

1. Sit in a chair, feet flat on the floor.

2. Inhale and slowly bring your left arm across your chest.

3. Place your right hand either above or below the left elbow.

4. Gently push on your arm. Do not force this movement. Feel the tension in the back of your upper arm and shoulder.

5. Hold for at least five seconds.

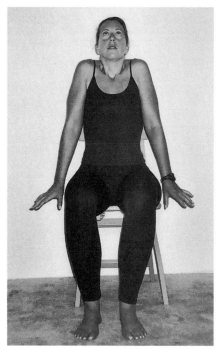

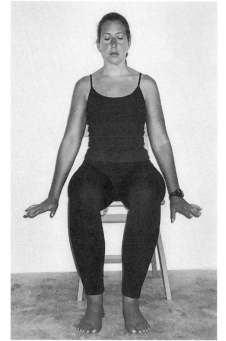

Raise shoulders toward ears.   Now push toward the floor.

6. Exhale slowly and relax.

7. Let your arms hang down by your sides while breathing in through your nose and out through your mouth.

8. Inhale and slowly bring your right arm across your chest.

9. Place your left hand either above or below the right elbow.

10. Gently push on your arm, without force.

11. Hold for at least five seconds.

12. Exhale slowly and lower your arms back to your sides.

13. Relax for 10 seconds.

14. Repeat 2 more times each side.

Triceps Stretch

1. Sit in a chair, feet shoulder width apart.

2. Breathe easily throughout this exercise.

3. Relax your head, neck and shoulders.

4. Bend and raise your right arm parallel to your right ear.

Left arm stretch.   And now the right.

5. Hold your right elbow with your left hand.

6. Gently pull your elbow behind your head in a downward motion. Do not force this; go only as far as you can without strain.

7. You should feel a slight stretch in your shoulder and the upper back of your arm.

8. Hold for five to ten seconds.

9. Bring your arm down and relax for five seconds.

10. Bend and raise your left arm parallel to your left ear.

11. Hold your left elbow with your right hand.

Chest Stretch Seated

1. Sit backward in a chair with legs on either side of chair back.

2. Arms are at your sides.

3. Breathe in through your nose and out through your mouth.

4. Inhale and bring your arms behind you.

5. Interlace your fingers.

6. Exhale and bring your arms up as far as your can, without strain, keeping shoulders relaxed.

7. Bring your shoulder blades together as far as you can. Do not force this movement.

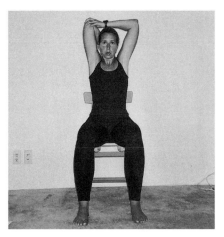

Bend and raise right arm.

And now the left arm.

8. Hold this position for five to ten seconds.

9. Slowly bring your arms back to your sides.

10. Breathe in through your mouth and out through your nose for 5 seconds.

11. Repeat two more times.

12. When you finish your last repetition, shake out your hands and wiggle your fingers.

Back Stretch Seated

1. Sit in a chair; feet flat on the floor, arms at your sides.

2. Inhale and raise arms parallel to the floor, interlacing your fingers.

3. Exhale, and at the same time, push palms outward and relax neck. Do not strain.

4. Hold for five to ten seconds and breathe easily.

6. Slowly raise your head and bring arms back to your sides.

7. Relax your head, neck and shoulders.

8. Repeat two more times.

Training Tip

Remember to release all stretches with control.

Feel your chest open.

Upper Body and Back Stretch

1. Stand facing the back of a chair.

2. Place hands on back of chair and move backward until arms are almost straight.

3. Inhale through your nose, and as you exhale, slowly bend from the waist until your head is in between your arms.

4. Keep your knees slightly bent.

5. Relax your head and neck.

6. Breathe easily and hold for five to ten seconds.

7. Slowly raise your upper body and relax for five seconds.

8. Repeat two more times.

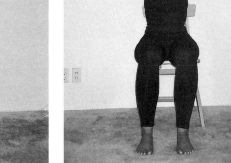

Interlace fingers . . .   . . . now push hands outward and stretch.

Hand and Wrist Stretch

1. Sit tall with your feet flat on the floor.

2. Relax your head, neck and shoulders.

3. Bring your right arm straight up in front of you.

4. With your left hand gently grasp the fingers of your right hand and gently bring your fingers back toward your body. Feel this stretch in the underside of your wrist.

5. Hold for five to ten seconds. Do not force these movements.

6. With your left hand, gently push the right hand down. Feel the stretch along the back of your hand and wrist.

7. Hold for five to ten seconds.

8. Relax with both hands in your lap for five seconds.

9. Bring your left arm straight up in front of you.

10. With your right hand, gently grasp the fingers of your left hand and gently bring your fingers back toward your body. Feel this stretch in the underside of your wrist.

11. Hold for five to ten seconds. Do not force these movements.

12. With your right hand, gently push the left hand down. Feel the stretch along the back of your hand and wrist.

13. Hold for five to ten seconds.

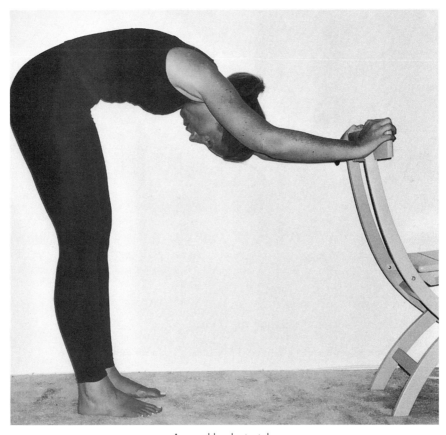

A good back stretch.

14. Gently shake out your hands and wiggle your fingers.

15. Repeat two more times each side.

Overall Body Stretch

1. Stand with legs shoulder width apart. Do not lock your knees.

2. Relax your head, neck and shoulders.

3. Take a deep breath in through your nose.

4. Bring your arms above your head.

5. Stand on your toes if you can; if not, remain flat-footed.

6. Reach for the sky.

7. Hold this position and keep reaching for 10 to 20 seconds, while breathing in through your nose and out through your mouth.

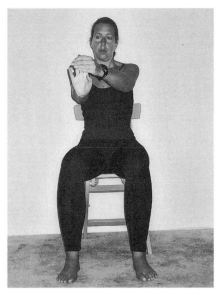

A gentle stretch for the right hand.

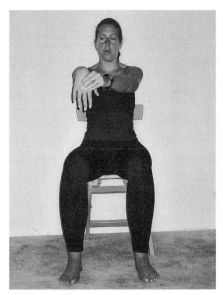

Stretch toward the floor.

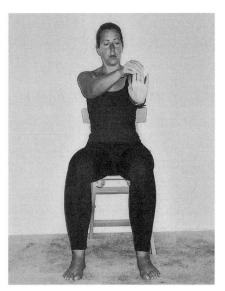

Now the left hand.

Stretch your wrist.

8. Exhale and slowly return your arms to your sides.

9. Relax for 10 seconds.

10. Repeat one more time.

Training Tip

When you're at a show, do the Overall Body Stretch during the day to ease physical tension.

Upper Body Stretch

Note: If you have knee problems, do not do this exercise.

1. Stand tall with your back against a wall.

2. Relax your head, neck and shoulders.

3. Breathe easily throughout this exercise.

4. Step away from the wall about one or two feet.

5. Feet are shoulder width apart, toes are pointed straight ahead.

6. Knees are slightly bent. Remember, do not lock your knees.

7. Slowly turn to the right from your waist until you can place both hands on the wall behind you. Hands should touch wall at shoulder height. If you cannot touch the wall, turn only as much as you can. Do not force this movement.

8. Hold for five to ten seconds and slowly turn back facing front.

9. Breathe and relax for five seconds.

10. Slowly turn to the left from your waist until you can place both hands on the wall behind you. Hands should touch wall at shoulder height. If you cannot touch the wall, turn only as much as you can. Do not force this movement.

11. Hold for five to ten seconds and slowly turn back facing front.

12. Breathe and relax for five seconds.

13. Repeat two more times each side.

Lower Body Stretch

1. Sit in a chair, feet flat on the floor, hands resting in your lap. Breathe in through your nose and out through your mouth.

2. Sit up tall and relax your head, neck and shoulders.

3. Cross your left leg over your right knee.

4. Inhale, and at the same time lean over, bringing your chest toward your lap. Do not force this movement.

Right side stretch.

Now the left side.

5. Place your hands on the left leg or allow them to dangle.

6. Exhale slowly while holding the stretch.

7. Hold for at least five seconds.

8. Inhale and slowly sit up, keeping your legs crossed.

9. Breathe in through your nose and out through your mouth.

10. Slowly rotate your left ankle to the right in a circle.

11. Reverse direction and rotate your ankle to the left in a circle.

12. When you've finished rotating, wiggle your toes.

13. Uncross your legs and relax for 10 seconds.

14. Cross your right leg over your left knee.

15. Sit up tall and relax your head, neck and shoulders.

16. Inhale and at the same time lean over, bringing your chest toward your lap.

17. Place your hands on your right leg or allow them to dangle.

18. Exhale slowly while holding the stretch.

19. Hold for at least five seconds.

20. Inhale and slowly sit up, keeping your legs crossed.

21. Breathe in through your nose and out through your mouth.

22. Slowly rotate your right ankle to the right in a circle.

23. Reverse direction and rotate your ankle to the left in a circle.

24. When you've finished rotating, wiggle your toes.

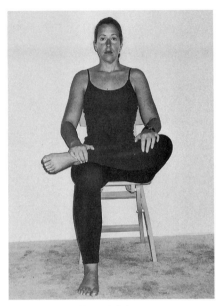

Cross left leg.

Bend and stretch.

Cross right leg.

Now stretch.

25. Uncross your legs and relax for 10 seconds.

26. Repeat two more times each side.

Hip Stretch

1. Sit in a chair, feet flat on the floor and hands resting in your lap.

2. Relax your head, neck and shoulders.

3. Put your hands around your left knee, exhale and raise it to your chest.

4. Keep your back straight but relaxed.

5. Hold for at least five seconds.

6. Inhale and slowly bring your leg back to the floor in a controlled motion.

7. Relax and sit back, hands in your lap, for 10 seconds.

8. Put your hands around your right knee, exhale and raise it to your chest.

Bring left leg up.   And now the right leg.

9. Keep your back straight but relaxed.

10. Hold for at least five seconds.

11. Inhale and slowly bring your leg back to the floor in a controlled motion.

12. Relax and sit back, hands in your lap, for 10 seconds.

13. Repeat two more times each side.

Thigh Stretch (Quads)

1. Stand one to two feet away from the back of a sturdy chair or use a wall.

2. Legs are together.

3. Breathe easily throughout this exercise.

4. Place your right hand on the back of the chair or wall. Bring your left leg back and hold your foot with your left hand.

5. Pull your heel toward your buttocks, without strain.

6. Hold for five to ten seconds and slowly lower your left leg. Relax your arms.

7. Place your left hand on the back of the chair or wall. Bend your right leg back and hold your foot with your right hand.

8. Gently pull your heel toward your buttocks, without strain.

Left leg, left hand.   Right leg, right hand.

9. Hold for five to ten seconds and slowly lower leg. Relax your arms.

10. Repeat two more times each side.

Inner Thigh and Side Stretch

1. Stand parallel to a chair with its seat facing your side. Make sure seat is at a comfortable height for your leg. (See photo.) Breathe easily throughout this exercise.

2. Carefully place your right foot on a chair. Straighten your right leg, without strain.

3. Keep your left leg on the floor, knee slightly bent, foot parallel to the chair.

4. Slowly bend to the right without strain; hands are at your sides. Feel the stretch in your right inner thigh.

5. Hold for five to ten seconds.

   Note: For an added side stretch, raise your hands overhead and slowly bend to the right. Do not strain. (See photo.)

6. Slowly return to a standing position and relax for five seconds.

7. Now, turn to your left side and carefully place your left foot on a chair. Straighten your left leg, without strain.

8. Keep your right leg on the floor, knee slightly bent, foot parallel to the chair.

9. Slowly bend to the left without strain; hands are at your sides. Feel the stretch in your left inner thigh.

10. Hold for five to ten seconds.

    Note: For an added side stretch, raise your hands overhead and slowly bend to the right. Do not strain.

11. Repeat two more times each side.

Calf Stretch

1. Stand with your hands on the back of a chair or wall.

2. Keep your back straight and relaxed.

3. Bring your right foot forward and bend the knee slightly.

4. Feet face forward throughout this exercise.

5. Keep your left leg straight, behind you, heel flat on the ground.

6. Take a deep breath in through your nose, and as you exhale through your mouth, slowly move your hips forward. Keep your lower back flat.

Right thigh and side stretch.   Left thigh and side stretch.

7. Your left heel remains flat on the floor. Feel the stretch in your left calf.

8. Hold for five to ten seconds.

9. Bring both legs together and relax for five seconds.

10. Move your left foot forward and bend the knee slightly.

11. Keep your right leg straight, behind you, heel flat on the ground.

12. Take a deep breathe in through your nose, and as you exhale through your mouth, slowly move your hips forward. Keep your lower back flat.

13. Your right heel remains flat on the floor. Feel the stretch in your right calf.

14. Hold for five to ten seconds.

15. Repeat two more times each side.

Shin and Calf Stretch

1. Sit in a chair, feet flat on the floor.

2. Exhale and slowly lift your left leg as far as you can without strain, pointing your toes. Do not lock your knee.

3. Hold for five to ten seconds.

4. Inhale and flex your toes. (Pull toes gently toward your body.)

5. Hold for at least five seconds.

Left calf stretch.

Right calf stretch.

6. Exhale and slowly lower your leg in a controlled motion.

7. Relax for five seconds.

8. Exhale and slowly lift your right leg as far as you can without strain, pointing your toes. Do not lock your knee.

9. Hold for five to ten seconds.

10. Inhale and flex your toes. (Pull toes gently toward your body.)

11. Hold for at least ten seconds.

12. Exhale and slowly lower your leg in a controlled motion.

13. Relax for 10 seconds.

14. Repeat two more times each side.

Hamstring Stretch

1. Stand facing the seat of a chair, making sure the seat is at a height comfortable for your leg. (See photo.)

2. Place your left heel on chair seat and straighten your leg, without strain.

3. Bend right knee slightly.

4. Inhale and bend forward, bringing your chest to your knee. Go as far as you can without strain.

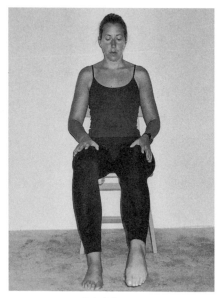

Lift left leg . . .

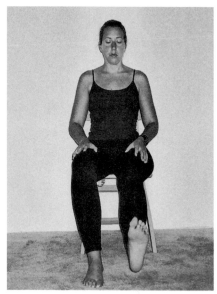

. . . now flex left foot.

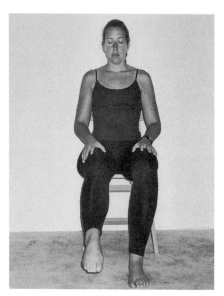

Lift right leg . . .

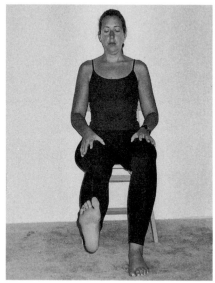

. . . and flex right foot.

5. Breathe easily and hold for five to ten seconds.

6. Slowly return to standing position.

7. Place your right heel on the chair seat and straighten your leg, without strain.

8. Bend left knee slightly.

Left leg stretch.

Right leg stretch.

9. Inhale and bend forward, bringing your chest to your knee, without strain.

10. Breathe easily and hold for five to ten seconds.

11. Slowly return to standing position.

12. Repeat two more times.

Cool Down Breath

1. Sit comfortably in a chair, feet flat on the floor and hands resting in your lap.

2. Breathe slowly in through your nose, keeping your breath deep and smooth, then exhale slowly and smoothly through your mouth.

3. Repeat two more times.

When you include stretching in a daily program, you'll see great results in how it eases ring nerves, increases energy levels and smooths your movements in the ring. Remember to stretch before and after every training class and in any competitive endeavor. Consider getting physical on a regular basis with aerobics or weight training. Take up a sport, become a walker, runner or biker. Make physical exercise a part of your life, to enhance your competitive edge.

Training Tip

Adapt the above stretches to use in your vehicle, in training class and at competitions.

Training Tip

Take Yoga or Pilates classes or use video programs to keep yourself fit, flexible and forever young. These exercises will also work wonders for your mental health.

FURTHER READING

Judith B. Alter. *Stretch and Strengthen* (reissue). Mariner Books, 1992.

Bob Anderson et al., *Stretching: 20th Anniversary.* Shelter Publications, 2003.

Mark Ansari and Liz Lark. *Yoga for Beginners (spiralbound).* Perennial, 1999.

Dr. Steven D. Stark. *The Stark Reality of Stretching: An Informed Approach for All Activities and Every Sport* (4th edition). Stark Reality Corp., 2000.

Pavel Tsatsouline. *Relax into Stretch: Instant Flexibility Through Mastering Muscle Tension.* Dragon Door Publication, 2001.

Pavel Tsatsouline. *Super Joints: Russian Longevity Secrets for Pain-Free Movement, Maximum Mobility and Flexible Strength.* Dragon Door Publication, 2001.

RESOURCE LIST

Stretching, http://www.stretching.com

Stretching and Sports Injury Solutions, http://www.thestretchinghandbook.com

Sports Coach-Static Stretching Exercises, http://www.brianmac.demon.co.uk/stretch.htm

The Physician and Sports Medicine: Myths and Truths of Stretching, http://www.physsportsmed.com/issues/2000/08_00/shrier.htm

Stretching FAQ by Brad Appleton, http://www.faqs.org/contrib/stretching

Column on Training, Stretching and Flexibility, http://www.stadion.com/column.html

Wrap-Up

Congratulations—you've done it! You've completed the Conquering Ring Nerves program and set your course to become a self-assured handler with a zest for competing. Maybe you worked chapter by chapter, or perhaps you took bits and pieces that interested you from the book to fit them into an existing training program. No matter what you've chosen, it is the discipline of practice that will create your success in the competitive dog show arena.

The handlers whose stories are featured in each chapter illustrate that even the most crippling ring nerve symptoms can be faced, coped with and overcome. You have everything within you to attain your highest goals. Instill the exercises and techniques into your daily life. You'll see great results and your dog will love you for it.

You can run with the big dogs or sit on the porch and bark.

Wallace Arnold

Happy training!
Diane

Appendix A

Full Body Progressive Relaxation: The Path to Serenity (script for recording)

Progressive Relaxation is a method wherein, working from head to toes, large muscle groups are tensed for a few seconds, then the tension is released and the muscle relaxes. This exercise will take you to a state of very deep relaxation. When practiced regularly, the effects of Progressive Relaxation include an overall decrease in anxiety, improvement in concentration and increased self-esteem. This exercise has been adapted from the Competing At Your Peak Audio Ring Nerve Program.

GUIDELINES FOR PROGRESSIVE RELAXATION

- Lie down or sit in a comfortable chair. Your arms are at your sides, fingers open; or cradle your hands in your lap.

- Keep your eyes closed throughout this exercise.

- Focus all of your attention on this exercise, and when your thoughts stray, look at them for a few moments, then gently refocus on the exercise.

- In the first part of the exercise, you will be tightening up large groups of muscles. Concentrate on the tension, study where you feel the tension and then, when I tell you to, relax.

- Hold the tension for a count of five to ten seconds. Adapt this to your comfort level.

- Release the tension for a count of 10 to 15 seconds. Adapt this to your comfort level.

- Remember, tighten the muscles but do not strain.

- Part two includes a soothing visualization.

The following script should be recorded slowly in a calming, soothing voice.

EXERCISE

1. Begin Yoga Breath and try to maintain it throughout this exercise. If you can't, breathe easily and naturally.

2. Put your toes together and gently push them down toward the floor.

3. Tighten your shin and calf muscles. Tighten your knees. Tense your thighs. Tense your buttocks. Look at the tightness and hold it. I want you to hold it, hold it, and now let go. Relax and feel the tension flow out.

4. Again, concentrate on your toes, and relax them. Relax the muscles of your legs and let the tension go. Relax your thighs, relax the muscles of your buttocks. Let all the tension go.

5. As I mention each part, concentrate on it and relax even more. Toes relaxed, shin and calf muscles relaxed, knees relaxed, legs and thighs relaxed, buttocks relaxed. You are feeling more and more relaxed.

6. Now we are going to work on your stomach muscles. Tighten up your stomach muscles; get them really tight. Focus on where you feel the tension and hold it. Now hold it, hold it, and now relax. I want you to feel the tension flow out while you relax your stomach. Let the tension go as your body sinks into your bed or chair. You're feeling more and more relaxed.

7. Again, relax your stomach muscles. Release all the tension in your stomach.

8. Tighten the muscles of your back. Arch and tense the small of your back. Hold it. Now hold the tension, and now let it go. Relax the muscles of your back, and let them go. Try to let your back melt into your bed or chair.

9. Feel your body getting more and more relaxed. Feel how heavy your body feels as you let all the tension go.

10. Now we are going to work on the muscles of your chest. Take a deep breath through your mouth and hold it for a few seconds. Focus on the tension in your chest. Slowly release your breath and feel all the tension in your chest flow out. Take long deep Yoga Breaths and if any spots of tension remain, let them flow out of your chest. Keep relaxing the muscles of your chest. You're feeling more and more relaxed.

11. Concentrate on each part again, and as I mention it you'll let any spots of tension go, and become more and more relaxed: stomach relaxed, back relaxed, feel yourself melt into your bed or chair. Your chest is relaxed and you are breathing easily and comfortably, feeling more and more relaxed.

12. To work on the muscles of your fingers, hands, arms and elbows, raise your arms slightly and splay your fingers. Hold it, hold it, and now slowly bring your arms back to your sides and relax your fingers. Let your arms go limp and feel the tension flow down along your arms, past your elbows, through your hands and out of your fingers. Your arms and hands feel heavy at your sides.

13. Shrug your shoulders and tense them. Hold the tension, hold it and now relax your shoulders and feel the tension flow out. Your shoulders feel very relaxed.

14. Gently pull your shoulder blades together and feel the tension. Hold it, hold it, and relax. Feel all the tension in your shoulders flow out.

15. As I say each part, look at it and make it even more relaxed: shoulders, arms and elbows, relax them. Hands and fingers are more relaxed. Find any spots of tension and let it go. You are feeling very relaxed.

16. Let's work on an area that holds a lot of tension, your neck muscles. Gently arch your neck and point your chin toward the ceiling. Feel the tension in the back of your neck muscles. Hold it, let it build up, but don't strain. Now let all the tension go and feel it flow out of your neck. Your head feels heavy on the bed or chair; you are more and more relaxed.

17. Now let's work on the face. Squeeze your eyes tightly shut. Wrinkle your nose and open your mouth very wide. Feel the tension in your face, your eyes, mouth, cheeks and jaw. Don't strain, but hold it. Hold it and now relax and feel the tension flow out of your face. Concentrate and relax all the muscles in your face, letting the tension go.

18. Check your body again for any signs of tension. As I say each part, try to let go of muscle tension even more. Remember, if stray thoughts distract you, let them be, then refocus on what you are doing.

19. Is there any tension in your feet, toes, legs, knees, shins or calf muscles? If there is, let the tension go. Look at your thighs and buttocks, concentrate on these muscles and let the tension go. Make them even more relaxed.

20. Is there any tension in your stomach, back or chest? If there is, take it one spot at a time and let it go.

21. Continue Yoga Breath and feel yourself relaxing more and more.

22. Check over your fingers, hands, elbows, arms and shoulders. If there is any tension, concentrate on it and let it go. Try to get your arms and hands to feel limp and heavy as your muscles relax more and more.

23. Now the muscles of your face. If there is any tension in it, let it go. Look at your forehead, eyes, nose, mouth and jaw. Relax them.

24. I want you to keep thinking how relaxed you are as you sink into your bed or chair. Now imagine that you are walking along a beautiful beach on a tropical island. The sand is white, the warm clear water laps at your ankles, and you feel completely relaxed and at peace. Your dog runs along by your side. You have no worries, no fears, you are completely at peace. If your mind wanders, gently bring it back to the beautiful beach.

25. While you walk along this beach, relax the muscles of your toes, feet, shins and calves. Relax the muscles of your legs, let the tension go. Relax your thighs and buttocks, let all the tension flow out of these parts of your body.

26. Keep picturing yourself on this beautiful beach with your dog, feeling calm and at peace and relax the muscles of your stomach. Relax your back, and let it melt into the bed or chair. Relax the muscles of your chest, feeling how light it is, while you breathe easily and comfortably.

27. Imagine yourself on that beautiful beach and relax the muscles of your fingers, hands and arms letting all the tension go. Relax your shoulders and your neck. Your head feels heavy and sinks into the bed or chair.

28. Relax all the muscles in your face. Feel how radiant your face is without the tension. Relax your face even more, and let all the tension flow out of your face.

29. Keep imagining yourself on that beautiful beach with the warm water lapping at your ankles, with the sun warming you and your beloved dog running alongside you. You're at peace and are able to enjoy all that life has to offer.

30. Keep seeing yourself on the beach and take one last look over your body. If any spots of tension exist, let them flow out. Keep relaxing your whole body, letting go of all the tension. Your body is heavy on the bed or chair, and your mouth hangs open. You are more and more relaxed, letting go of all the tension, letting it flow out of you. You feel calm and serene. Continue to let go of all the tension until every part of your body is deeply relaxed. Keep breathing and letting go. Your whole body feels relaxed and serene, relaxed and calm.

31. Keep relaxing and as I count to three, slowly sit up and see how good you feel. One . . . two . . . three.

Appendix B

Quickie Stress-Buster

When you don't have time for Full-Body Progressive Relaxation, use this great tension reliever adapted from the Competing At Your Peak Audio Ring Nerve Program. At a show, you can do this stress-buster in your car, the bathroom, or while waiting for your turn in the ring.

In this exercise, instead of tensing separate muscles and then releasing the tension, you'll tighten your whole body at once, then let go of the tension in one shot. Remember, you want to tighten your muscles, but do so without strain.

EXERCISE

1. Sit in a chair, hands cradled in your lap; or lie down, arms relaxed at your sides.

2. Eyes are closed. When your thoughts stray, calmly refocus on the exercise. Tighten up all the muscles in your body at once:

3. Push your toes away from you.

4. Tighten your legs, buttocks and stomach muscles.

5. Tense your arms and elbows. Make a fist with each hand.

6. Tighten your chest, shoulders, neck and head.

7. Wrinkle your nose and clench your jaw.

8. Hold the tension for five to ten seconds.

9. Exhale and relax your entire body.

10. Feel the tension flow out of every muscle and limb.

11. Keep breathing easily and letting go of all the tension in your body.

12. In your mind's eye, look around your body for any spots of tension, and let them go.

13. Keep breathing and releasing body tension for another 10 to 15 seconds.

Appendix C

Guided Imagery: Dream It and Do It (script for recording)

Guided imagery is a wonderful technique that allows you to rehearse your perfect event while feeling calm and collected in the safety of your home. In Part I, you'll imagine yourself during preshow preparations, from sending in your entry to entering the show ring. In Part II, you'll visualize yourself and your dog in a perfect performance. Since this script if for a general audience, you'll have to imagine your personal details as we go along.

Either lie down or sit in a comfortable chair for this exercise. As you hear the word *calm* throughout this visualization, make it a point to relax your body. Try listening to the Progressive Relaxation recording right before doing this exercise, to get into a deeply relaxed state.

The following script is to be recorded in a soft but upbeat voice. Emphasize the word *calm* with a deep, but soothing tone. The script has been adapted from the Competing At Your Peak Audio Ring Nerve Program.

EXERCISE PART I

1. You get your premium list in the mail and decide to enter the show. You are excited about competing and feel relaxed and *calm*.

2. You fill out the entry form, write out the check and as you slip it into the mailbox, you say, "I can't wait to compete in this show." You are confident and *calm*.

3. In the weeks before the show, you and your dog work hard in training sessions. Things are coming together for both of you and he's looking good. He is as eager as you are about competing. You both feel excited and *calm*.

4. Every day you practice some part of the Ring Nerve Program to keep yourself sharp. Your confidence increases because you have many tools to keep you focused and *calm* no matter what happens during your routine.

5. The day before the show, you check out the map, figure out how to get to the show site, and are looking forward to the challenge competing gives you. You feel *calm*.

6. You groom your dog for the show, and you're both having fun, feeling relaxed and easy and *calm*.

7. The night before, you pick out your clothes, pack up the car, cut up the goodies for your dog and make sure you have everything you need. You feel energized about getting into the ring to compete and feel *calm*.

8. You get to bed early, do Yoga Breathing before drifting off to sleep and wake feeling refreshed and energetic, focused on what you have to do and you are *calm*.

9. You and your dog eat a good breakfast, you pack your dog in the car and drive to the show site. You enjoy the car ride. Your energy is high, yet you remain relaxed and *calm*.

10. When you pull into the parking lot you feel excited about showing and can't wait to get into the ring, and you are *calm*.

11. You potty your dog and he is alert, eager and very attentive. This is going to be fun, he's thinking. You are *calm* and he knows it.

12. You check in, pick up your number, find your ring and check to make sure you know when you'll be called. The environment is noisy and filled with tension from other handlers and their dogs, but you remain relaxed and confident and *calm*. Your dog follows your lead, and plays it cool.

13. You check out your ring and watch the judge and other competitors, and your confidence is rising. You are *calm*.

14. You warm up your dog and he's paying close attention to you. He feels your *calmness* and knows you are completely with him.

15. You keep your eye on the running order, and it's almost your turn. Your excitement is building, and you are eager to compete and you feel *calm*.

16. You are at ringside right on time and wait in the on-deck position. Your dog is right with you, and both of you are excited and alert and *calm*.

17. You're up! You and your dog enter the ring feeling up to the challenge, eager, focused, confident and *calm*.

PART II

1. You enter the ring with high confidence and determination, and feel completely balanced in mind and body. You are able to focus intently on your dog and event. You feel *calm*.

2. You see in your imagination each aspect of your event, clearly and in detail. As you and your dog move around the ring, your body is relaxed, yet you feel vibrant and alive. You are enjoying every moment and your dog puts all of his attention and focus on you as he completes each part of the course or routine effortlessly. Both of you are competing with enthusiasm and *calm*.

3. You and your dog are a team, sharing and communicating in a common language, and throughout your event you both are alert, focused on each other and *calm*.

4. As you move throughout your event, there is no audience, no noise, no judges, no other handlers, just you and your dog and both of you perform perfectly. You are relaxed and *calm*.

5. See in your mind's eye you and your dog moving effortlessly through your event. You are centered in mind and body and nothing and no one can shake you. You have complete command of yourself, your dog and your event.

6. Visualize yourself and your dog moving in perfect harmony and finishing with an outstanding performance, achieving the success you want and can have.

Appendix D

Ring Nerve Desensitization Program

WHAT IS A DESENSITIZATION PROGRAM?

Systematic Desensitization is an effective, popular behavioral treatment for anxiety and phobias, first clinically used in the 1950s by Dr. Joseph Wolpe. In this method, a person who responds with emotional discomfort and panic to certain situations, things or people is taught to relax deeply and then progress through two stages. First, in Fantasy Desensitization, they visualize facing their fears while in this calm condition. Visualization is practiced repeatedly until the dreaded situation, thing or person no longer provokes an anxious response. When the person feels ready, they face their fears in the real situation, Reality Desensitization, and in most cases find that that their anxiety level has dropped and their coping skills have increased.

Systematic Desensitization is counterconditioning. You reduce your conditioned response, in this case, anxiety, by creating a desirable or incompatible response, which is relaxation. And the great news is that if you are truly in a state of deep relaxation, it is physiologically impossible to be anxious.

The desensitization process also involves breaking down big overwhelming fears into many very small manageable steps, then constructing a "ring nerve hierarchy," rating each step on the Ring Nerve Anxiety Scale and then listing the steps from easiest to most difficult, and finally charting your step-by-step progress. One at a time, each step is faced (practicing many times if necessary), while using the various exercises and techniques in the ring nerve program, until the situation can be encountered without a panicky reaction.

GUIDELINES TO DESENSITIZE YOURSELF

1. You must be able to relax quickly on command and stay in that state for a period through breathing or other calming techniques. Review all chapters and Appendix A, *Full Body Progressive Relaxation*.

2. Be able to visualize all the details of your feared situations.

3. Be sure you have created a *safe space*, and can bring it up instantly to reduce anxiety. Review Chapter 5: Blue Skies, the Beam and the Bubble.

4. Be sure you have created a hierarchy of fears that contain clearly detailed steps that are easily measurable for progress.

5. Do not skip a step. As your confidence increases, this commonly occurs. It's best to work each step until it holds no fear for you.

6. Begin with Fantasy Desensitization first for the following reasons:

    •   It will allow you to review and practice the exercises in this program.

    •   You will find out which techniques reduce your anxiety the fastest without leaving the safety of your home.

    •   Some steps will be hard to practice until you're doing the real thing, but Fantasy Desensitization will go a long way in reducing ring nerves.

    •   You will be better prepared for Reality Desensitization.

7. You take control of your anxiety by making the decision to begin Reality Desensitization only when you are ready.

8. Setbacks are normal. All desensitization, whether Fantasy or Reality, takes determination, practice and patience, and you'll encounter bumps along the way. For example, it's common to have anxiety appear in a situation that you think you've worked through. You might have to go back and practice on a previous step. Don't worry if you do; you're still moving ahead and making progress.

9. Do not set a time frame in which you must meet your goal. That is a sure way to set yourself up to fail.

10. Reinforce yourself with something special along the way, not just when you've reached your goal, but for the effort you're making as well as each small step you've completed.

11. Practice every day. If you don't have time to practice at length, at least review calming exercises and do a short visualization. Stopping for any length of time will impede your progress.

12. Review relaxation techniques at least once a week so they will work quickly when you need them.

13. Measure your level of anxiety on the Ring Nerve Anxiety Scale on each completed step, to see your progress.

14. Chart your progress so you can see how far you've come, using the pages in this section or your Ring Nerve Journal.

15. You may decide to desensitize yourself with the support of someone you trust. This can be very helpful, but remember that you are the master of your program and they must listen to your needs.

CREATING YOUR RING NERVE HIERARCHY

1. Set a clear, defined goal that you want to reach.

2. Break down your goal into as many tiny pieces as possible. You want to make each step possible to achieve, to increase your confidence.

3. List a minimum of 10 steps for each goal.

4. Rate each step on the Ring Nerve Anxiety Scale, so you know your starting point.

5. List the steps from easiest to most difficult.

6. Reread the exercises from previous chapters to guide you.

A HANDLER'S TALE

Lisa says, "It was easy to write down my main fear, but as I began to think about and write down all the little things that make up the fear of competing in Agility, I was actually surprised at how many steps I came up with. I think when you live with fear, it becomes almost natural and you don't realize the scope of it until you take a close look at the details. It floored my when I faced how afraid I was to practice with my dogs at home right before a show. I have a course set up in a field on my farm, right next to the yard where I play with my dogs. When I set up a practice time I would get tense, and my dogs would tense up too, and this was at home! Or I would get busy and blow off practicing. I thought I was busy or something that I had to do always took my time away; little did I know how I avoided my practice course because I was so afraid. Then one day, right before a trial, I had a panic attack as I looked out my window at the field with the practice course. Soon after that, I started to have panic when I walked my dogs from my yard into the field. In the field my anxiety would spike, the dogs would pick up on it and practice times became an ordeal."

Lisa's main fear was "competing in an Agility trial," but that was too big to work on initially. We decided first to tackle her fear of the practice course she had set up in her field, and then when she decreased her anxiety during practice, we would create another hierarchy for competing at an agility trial.

Following is Lisa's Ring Nerve Hierarchy, including ratings from the Ring Nerve Anxiety Scale. Lisa's Handler's Tale appeared in Chapter 5, "Creating a Safe Space."

My Ring Nerve Hierarchy

Fantasy_____ Reality_____ Date Begun_____ Date Completed_____

Main Fear: *Practicing in my field*

1. Looking out the window at the yard next to your field. Rating: *0*

2. Going out into the yard with your dogs. Rating: *1*

3. Playing in your yard with your dogs. Rating: *1*

4. Looking out the window at your field without a course in it. Rating: *3*

5. Walking your dogs into the field with no course in it. Rating: *4 1/2*

6. Standing with your dogs in a field that has no course. Rating: *5 1/2*

7. Playing with your dogs in the field with no course. Rating: *5 1/2*

8. Looking out the window at your field with the course set up in it. Rating: *7*

9. Walking your dogs into your field with the practice course set up. Rating: *8*

10. Standing in the field with your dogs near the course. Rating: *8 1/2*

11. Playing in the field with your dogs near the Agility equipment. Rating: *8 1/2*

12. Walking around each piece of equipment without touching anything. Rating: *9*

13. Walking around the course with your dogs while you touch each piece of equipment. Rating: *9 1/2*

14. Practicing with your dogs on only one piece of equipment. Rating: *10*

    Note: When the anxiety lessens (this could take some time), add another obstacle, until you are visualizing practicing the entire course with very little or no anxiety.

Lisa practiced diligently and when she was ready, she repeated the hierarchy by really doing each step over a period of many weeks.

A Handler's Tale (continued)

Lisa says, "I practiced Yoga Breath every day and got to a point where I could feel my whole body begin to calm down after only one breath. I found it best to practice my visualizations lying down and right after I had done the Progressive Relaxation. If I didn't have time for the whole exercise, then the Quickie Stress-Buster got me relaxed pretty quickly. It took me almost two months of daily visualizing before I felt ready to challenge myself and really get into the field with the dogs. I've had some setbacks; for example, my anxiety spiked while I was practicing a run with one of my dogs because I was thinking about entering a trial. I decided not to enter after that, and instead reviewed the Go With the Flow techniques from Chapter 4 for a few weeks.

"I've been competing again and my ring nerve symptoms are way down on the anxiety scale. Since I practice the exercises as much as possible, whatever technique I use usually kicks in right away. I've been doing the ring nerve program for some time and I don't have to fumble around trying to figure out what to use. I know exactly what exercises work for me and where and when. If anxiety hits and I feel it is getting to be a chronic problem, I just make a hierarchy and desensitize myself all over again. I feel that I've taken complete control of my anxiety."

Create your hierarchy in the form below. Copy the form to create other hierarchies, or write them down in your Ring Nerve Journal. Then rank them on the Ring Nerve Anxiety Scale.

My Ring Nerve Hierarchy

Fantasy_____ Reality_____ Date Begun_____ Date Completed_____

Main Fear _____

1. Rating:_____

2. Rating:_____

3. Rating:_____

4. Rating:_____

5. Rating:_____

6. Rating:_____

7. Rating:_____

8. Rating:_____

9. Rating:_____

10. Rating:_____

11. Rating:_____

12. Rating:_____

13. Rating:_____

14. Rating:_____

15. Rating:_____

16. Rating:_____

17. Rating:_____

18. Rating:_____

19. Rating:_____

20. Rating:_____

Sample of Ring Nerve Hierarchy

The following is the Fantasy hierarchy of a handler in Obedience, who was afraid of authority figures. In this case, even thinking about the judge looking at her made her heart pound. After many months of practice in Fantasy, she created a Reality hierarchy and was able to begin competing.

Main Fear: The judge

1. Look at a picture of a judge in a dog magazine.

2. Go to show, do not compete, but stand outside of ring and look at the judge.

3. Be inside the ring with the judge on other side of ring.

4. Walk toward the judge.

5. Stand next to the judge.

6. Enter Match Show.

7. Before the show starts, ask the judge a question.

8. Stand at ringside watching the judging of other handlers.

9. Wait in the on-deck position.

Ring Nerve Anxiety Scale

10_____ Panic city!!!

9_____ How do I get off this runaway train?!

8_____ No place to run, no place to hide

7_____ They're he-e-ere!

6_____ Not feeling so hot

5_____ Feel the build

4_____ Uh-oh!

3_____ First twinges

2_____ So far so good

1_____ Feelin' pretty cool

0_____ No ring nerves in sight

10. Have the judge ask if you are "ready."

11. Answer back "yes."

12. The judge calls the instructions.

13. Do your routine, listening to the judge's commands.

14. Finish and leave the ring.

Writing down your progress is an important part of this program. You may copy the form below, or keep track of your gains in your Ring Nerve Journal.

Charting My Ring Nerve Desensitization Progress

Fantasy_____ Reality_____ Date Begun_____ Date Completed_____

Main Goal: _____

Step #1: _____

What exercises and techniques did I use? _____

_____

What exercises and techniques worked? _____

_____

What didn't work? _____

_____

What additional steps do I have to take? _____

_____

Comments: _____

_____

Step #2: _____

What exercises and techniques did I use? _____

_____

What exercises and techniques worked? _____

_____

What didn't work? _____

_____

What additional steps do I have to take? _____

_____

Comments: _____
_____

Step # 3: _____

What exercises and techniques did I use? _____
_____

What exercises and techniques worked? _____
_____

What didn't work? _____
_____

What additional steps do I have to take? _____
_____

Comments: _____
_____

Step # 4: _____

What exercises and techniques did I use? _____
_____

What exercises and techniques worked? _____
_____

What didn't work? _____
_____

What additional steps do I have to take? _____
_____

Comments: _____
_____

Step # 5: _____

What exercises and techniques did I use? _____
_____

What exercises and techniques worked? _____
_____

What didn't work? _____
_____

What additional steps do I have to take? _____

_____

Comments: _____

_____

    Photocopy the form below:

CHARTING MY RING NERVE DESENSITIZATION PROGRESS

Fantasy_____ Reality_____ Date Begun_____ Date Completed_____

Main Goal: _____

Charting My Ring Nerve Desensitization Progress

Fantasy_____ Reality_____ Date Begun_____ Date Completed_____

Main Goal: _____

Step #: _____

What exercises and techniques did I use? _____

_____

What exercises and techniques worked? _____

_____

What didn't work? _____

_____

What additional steps do I have to take? _____

_____

Comments: _____

_____

_____

    If your ring nerves are severe, if you've stopped competing or thinking about doing so, begin the Ring Nerve Desensitization Program. Create a hierarchy of fears, and use the exercises and techniques you've learned in this book, first in the safety of Fantasy Desensitization, and then when you're ready venture out into Reality Desensitization. Work this program at your own pace and slowly, step by step, you'll get back into the competition. Start today. You can do it!

Appendix E

The Training Diary

The Training Diary (adapted from the *Audio Ring Nerve Program Training Manual* by Competing At Your Peak) is a very important part of your ring nerve program. By writing down the details of your experiences at competitions, you'll get an overall view of the mental and physical aspects of your performance and observe what exercises are effective and where. You'll be able to see your progress over time. It's only when you can look back on where you were that you can see how far you've come.

Each page is divided into several parts:

- **Identifying Information**: Who, What, When, Where

- **Goals for Today:** Write down what you want to achieve at this event. Use the goal-setting chapter to guide you.

- **How Did I Feel?** Record your ring nerve symptoms, and thoughts, feelings and emotions experienced during preshow preparations, warm-ups and during your event. Be sure to include post performance reactions.

- **What Worked?** Set down the details of your successes, both big and small.

  For example: "I'm actually calming down, and she got her first leg!" "We NQ'd, but she didn't shut down and we stayed connected!"

- **What Needs Work?** Document the aspects of your performance that need improvement, for the sole purpose of setting goals for future training sessions.

- **What Exercises and Techniques Did I Use?** List what exercises you used, in what circumstances, and how effective they were.

- **Goals Met:** Log what you accomplished. If you were not able to achieve your full goals, write down what you did do. No matter how small, it counts too.

Please photocopy the Training Diary pages, and add them to your Ring Nerve Journal.

THE TRAINING DIARY

Date:_____ Event:_____

Location:_____ Dog's name(s):_____

Goals for Today: _____

_____

_____

How Did I Feel? _____

_____

_____

_____

What Worked? _____

_____

_____

_____

_____

What Needs Work? _____

_____

_____

_____

_____

What Exercises and Techniques Did I Use? _____

_____

_____

_____

_____

Goals Met: _____

_____

_____

Notes: _____

_____

_____

_____

_____

Index